Englisch lernen mit **Berlitz**®

Just ask
Inspector Rebus

W0193877

Berlitz Publishing

München • New York • Singapur

Berlitz Englisch lernen mit Ian Rankin
Just ask Inspector Rebus

Vokabelerklärungen und Übungen: Helen Galloway
Layout: Ute Weber
Cover-Gestaltung: Dominik Lommer
Projektleitung: Eva Betz

© 2008 Berlitz Publishing, München

Englische Originalausgabe:
Beggars Banquet by Ian Rankin
Copyright © 2002 John Rebus Limited
First published by The Orion Publishing Group, London.

This edition is published by arrangement with Orion.

Berlitz Publishing
Mies-van-der-Rohe-Straße 1
D-80807 München

Satz: Franzis print&media, München
Druck: CS-Druck Cornelsen Stürtz, Berlin
Bindung: Stein + Lehmann, Berlin
Printed in Germany
ISBN 978-3-468-79232-8

1. 2. 3. 4. 5.   12 11 10 09 08

Inhalt

Lieber Krimi-Fan,

mit den spannenden Kurzkrimis von Ian Rankin halten Sie endlich ein Englischbuch in der Hand, das Sie garantiert nicht mehr weglegen wollen. Und vor lauter Nervenkitzel merken Sie vielleicht gar nicht, dass Sie ganz nebenbei auch Ihre Englischkenntnisse gehörig auffrischen und erweitern.

Damit Ihr Lesevergnügen nicht durch das Nachschlagen unbekannter Wörter gemindert wird, sind die schwierigsten Vokabeln im Text blau markiert und in der Marginalspalte übersetzt. Interessante Wörter, die in einer Infobox erklärt werden, sind zusätzlich mit einem Sternchen gekennzeichnet. Alle übersetzten Wörter sind außerdem im Wörterverzeichnis im Anhang zusammengefasst.

Allein beim Schmökern in den Krimis können Sie sehr viel dazulernen. Vielleicht möchten Sie aber auch Ihr Grammatikwissen und Ihre Vokabelkenntnisse zusätzlich erweitern oder aber Ihr Textverständnis prüfen. Zu diesem Zweck finden Sie auf jeder Seite knifflige und unterhaltsame Übungen. Die Vokabeln aus dem Text werden dort noch einmal verwendet und bleiben dadurch viel besser im Gedächtnis haften – so können Sie später leichter darauf zurückgreifen. Selbstverständlich sind auch die Lösungen zu allen Übungen im Anhang abgedruckt.

Und nun wünschen wir Ihnen viel Spaß und Spannung beim Lesen!

Ihre Berlitz-Redaktion

Death Is Not The End

One

Is loss redeemed by memory? Or does memory merely swell the sense of loss, becoming the enemy? The language of loss is the language of memory: remembrance, memorial, memento. People leave our lives all the time: some we met only briefly, others we'd known since birth. They leave us memories – which become skewed through time – and little more.

ausgeglichen •
bloß

Denkmal • Andenken

verzerrt

The silent dance continued. Couples writhed and shuffled, threw back their heads or ran hands through their hair, eyes darting around the dance floor, seeking out future partners maybe, or past loves to make jealous. The TV monitor gave a greasy look to everything.
No sound, just pictures, the tape cutting from dance floor to main bar to second bar to toilet hallway, then

krümmten sich •
schoben sich über
die Tanzfläche •
huschten … hin
und her • Tanz-
fläche •
schmierig

Auf welches Wort oder welchen Satz im Text beziehen sich
die folgenden Erklärungen?

Übung 1

1. the faculty which allows you to remember things
2. a statue or stone which is erected to remind people of
an event or famous person
3. something you buy or keep to remember an occasion
4. to walk with short, slow, dragging steps
5. to move quickly with short, sharp movements
6. to look for

entrance foyer, exterior front and exterior back. Exterior back was a puddled alley, full of rubbish bins and a Merc belonging to the club's owner. Rebus had heard about the alley: a punter had been knifed there the previous summer. Mr Merc had complained about the bloody smear on his passenger-side window. The victim had lived.

The club was called Gaitanos, nobody knew why. The owner just said it sounded American and a bit jazzy. The larger part of the clientele had decided on the nickname 'Guisers', and that was what you heard in the pubs on a Friday and Saturday night – 'Going down Guisers later?' The young men would be dressed smart-casual, the women scented from heaven and all stations south. They left the pubs around ten or half past – that's when it would be starting to get lively at Guisers.

Rebus was seated in a small uncomfortable chair which itself sat in a stuffy dimly lit room. The other chair was filled by an audio-visual technician, armed with two remotes. His occasional belches – of which he seemed blissfully ignorant – bespoke a recent snack of spring onion crisps and Irn-Bru.

Margin glossary:
- Gasse voller Pfützen • Mercedes • Kerl • niedergestochen
- Kundschaft •
- Spitzname •
- gehst du ins …
- sportlich elegant
- • hochgradig parfümiert
- muffig • schwach beleuchtet •
- Fernbedienungen
- • Rülpser •
- verrieten •
- (eine Art Limo)

Übung 2 Sind die folgenden Aussagen wahr oder falsch?
Tragen Sie ein T für true oder ein F für false in die Kästchen ein.

1. The alley behind Guisers was empty.
2. The owner of the Mercedes was very concerned about the person who was knifed.
3. Most of the customers at Gaitanos had renamed it Guisers.
4. The club only gets busy in the latter half of the evening.
5. The audio-visual technician is very embarrassed about his belching.

'I'm really only interested in the main bar, foyer and out front,' Rebus said.

'I could edit them down to another tape, but we'd lose definition. The recording's duff enough as it is.' The technician scratched inside the sagging armpit of his black T-shirt. Rebus leaned forward a little, pointing at the screen. 'Coming up now.' They waited. The view jumped from back alley to dance floor. 'Any second.' Another cut: main bar, punters queuing three deep. The technician didn't need to be told, and froze the picture. It wasn't so much black and white as sepia, the colour of dead photographs. Interior light, the audio-visual wizard had explained. He was adjusting the tracking now, and moving the action along one frame at a time. Rebus moved in on the screen, bending so one knee rested on the floor. His finger was touching a face. He took out the assortment of photos from his pocket and held them against the screen.

'It's him,' he said. 'I was pretty sure before. You can't go in a bit closer?'

'For now, this is as good as it gets. I can work on it later, stick it on the computer. The problem is the source material, to wit: one shitty security video.'

sie schneiden und auf ein anderes Video übertragen • Bildschärfe • beschissen • Achsel

mit Kunden brechend voll • hielt … an • Innenbeleuchtung • Genie • regelte • Einzelbild • stellte sich näher an

nämlich

Die folgende Zusammenfassung des Textes auf dieser Seite enthält drei sachliche Fehler. Können Sie sie finden und korrigieren?

Übung 3

Rebus and the technician are watching the security video from the nightclub. The quality of the tape couldn't be better. The tape shows the back alley, then the dance floor and then the main bar where there are very few people waiting to be served. Rebus gets closer to the screen and compares the image of a man with a single photograph which he has brought with him. He thinks he has identified the man.

Rebus sat back on his chair. 'All right,' he said. 'Let's run forward at half-speed.'

The camera stayed with the main bar for another fifteen seconds, then switched to the second bar and all *points on the compass*. When it returned to the main bar, the *crush* of drinkers seemed not to have moved. *Unbidden*, the technician froze the tape again.

'He's not there,' Rebus said. Again he approached the screen, touched it with his finger. 'He should be there.' 'Next to the *sex goddess*.' The technician belched again.

Yes. Spun silver hair, almost like a cloud of *candy-floss*, dark eyes and lips. While those around her *were* either *intent on* catching the eyes of the *bar staff* or on the dance floor, she was looking off to one side. There were no shoulders to her dress.

'Let's check the foyer,' Rebus said.

Twenty seconds there showed a steady stream entering the club, but no one leaving. Exterior front showed a queue awaiting *admittance* by the *brace* of *bouncers*, and a few passers-by.

'In the toilet maybe,' the technician suggested. But Rebus had studied the tape a dozen times already, and

Margin glossary:

Himmelsrichtungen • Gedränge • unaufgefordert

Sexbombe

Zuckerwatte • eifrig damit beschäftigt waren • Barpersonal

Einlass • Paar • Türsteher

Übung 4   Welche der Adjektive in der folgenden Liste beschreiben die Frau an der Bar?

- stunning
- bald
- unattractive
- distracted
- straight-haired
- warmly-dressed
- talkative

though he watched just once more he knew he
wouldn't see the young man again, not at the bar, not
on the dance floor, and not back around the table
where his mates were waiting – with increasing disbe-
lief and impatience – for him to get his round in. The
young man's name was Damon Mee and, according to
the timer running at the bottom right-hand corner of
the screen, he had vanished from the world sometime
between 11.44 and 11.45 p.m. on Friday 22 April.
'Where is this place anyway? I don't recognise it.'
'Kirkcaldy*,' Rebus said.
The technician looked at him. 'How come it ended up
here?'
Good question, Rebus thought, but not one he was
about to answer. 'Go back to that bar shot,' he said.
'Take it nice and slow again.'
The technician aimed his right-hand remote. 'Yes, sir,
Mr DeMille*,' he said.

April meant still not quite spring in Edinburgh. A few
sunny days to be sure, buds getting twitchy, wondering if winter had been paid the ransom. But there was
snow still hanging in a sky the colour of chicken bones.

Kumpels •
dass er eine
Runde schmiss •
Uhr

Wie kommt es,
dass ...?

zielte mit

Knospen • un-
ruhig • Lösegeld

Die Hafenstadt Kirkcaldy liegt an der Ostküste Schottlands
am Firth of Forth, der Mündung des Flusses Forth in die Nordsee.
Am gegenüberliegenden Ufer des Mündungsarms befindet sich
die Hauptstadt Edinburgh.
Der Techniker spielt hier auf das berühmte Zitat „All right,
Mr DeMille, I'm ready for my close-up" aus dem Schwarzweiß-
Film Sunset Boulevard (1950) an, der ähnlich schummrige
Lichtverhältnisse aufweist wie das Sicherheitsvideo. Norma
Desmond signalisiert dem Regisseur-Darsteller DeMille mit
diesem Satz, dass sie bereit für die Kamera ist.

wieder Meister werden

eine halbe Chance haben • bildete einen wesentlichen Bestandteil von • eine schnelle Nummer • Boulevardzeitung • Kriminalwachtmeisterin • sie überredete • trüb • Rasen • Zuschauer • unverbesserlich • Nähe

Schlusspfiff-Umarmung

Office talk: how Rangers* were going to retain the championship; why Hearts* and Hibs* would never win it – was it finally time for the two local sides to become friends, form one team which might – *might* – stand half a chance? As someone said, their rivalry was part and parcel of the city's make-up. Hard to imagine Rangers and Celtic* thinking of marriage in the same way, or even of a quick poke on the back stairs.

After years of following football only on pub televisions and in the back of the daily tabloid, Rebus was starting to go to matches again. DC Siobhan Clarke was to blame, coaxing him to a Hibs game one dreary afternoon. The men on the green sward weren't half as interesting as the spectators, who proved by turns sharp-witted, vulgar, perceptive and incorrigible. Siobhan had taken him to her usual spot. Those in the vicinity seemed to know her pretty well. It was a good-humoured afternoon, even if Rebus couldn't have said who scored the eventual three goals. But Hibs had won: the final-whistle hug from Siobhan was proof of that.

It was interesting to Rebus that, for all the barriers around the ground, this was a place where shields were dropped. After a while, it felt like one of the safest

info

Fußball gilt überall in Großbritannien als Nationalsport, aber in Schottland ist er ganz besonders populär. Als Folge dieser Leidenschaft haben sich große Rivalitäten zwischen den verschiedenen Mannschaften in Edinburgh und Glasgow entwickelt. Und es geht dabei nicht nur um Sport. Die Rivalitäten gehen auf die religiösen Probleme zurück, die diese Städte spalten. Die Anhänger von Glasgow Rangers und Hearts in Edinburgh sind traditionell evangelisch, während die Fans von Celtic in Glasgow und Hibernian (oder Hibs) in Edinburgh meist katholisch sind.

places he'd ever been. He recalled fixtures his father had taken him to in the fifties and early sixties – Cowdenbeath home games, and a crowd numbered in the hundreds; getting there necessitated a change of buses, Rebus and his younger brother fighting over who could hold the roll of tickets. Their mother was dead by then and their father was trying to carry on much as before, like they might not notice she was missing. Those Saturday trips to the football were supposed to fill a gap. You saw a lot of fathers and sons on the terraces but not many mothers, and that in itself was reminder enough. There was a boy of Rebus's age who stood near them. Rebus had walked over to him one day and blurted out the truth.

'I don't have a mum at home.'

The boy had stared at him, saying nothing.

Ever since, football had reminded him of those days and of his mother. He stood on the terraces alone these days and followed the game mostly – movements which could be graceful as ballet or as jagged as free association – but sometimes found that he'd drifted elsewhere, to a place not at all unpleasant, and all the time surrounded by a community of bodies and wills.

Spiele

Heimspiele •
erforderte

weiterzumachen

eine Lücke zu
füllen •
Ränge • allein
das war Erinnerung genug •
platzte mit ...
heraus

elegant • jäh

Beantworten Sie die Fragen zum Text.

Übung 5

1. How did Rebus travel to football matches as a boy?
2. What was the purpose of the trips to the football matches after Rebus's mother died?
3. What did the boy say when Rebus told him that his mother was dead?
4. Does Rebus ever get distracted from watching the football nowadays?

und sprach zu	'I'll tell you how to beat Rangers,' he said now, addressing the whole office. 'How?' Siobhan Clarke offered. 'Clone Stevie Scoular half a dozen times.'
	There were murmurs of agreement, and then the
steckte ... den	Farmer put his head around the door.
Kopf zur Tür	'John, my office.'
herein •	
Hauptkommissar	The Farmer – Chief Superintendent Watson to his
• offiziell	face – was pouring a mug of coffee from his machine when Rebus knocked at the open door.
winkte	'Sit down, John.' Rebus sat. The Farmer motioned with an empty mug, but he turned down the offer and wait-
bis sein	ed for his boss to get to his chair and the point both.
Chef zu seinem	'My birthday's coming up,' the Farmer said. This was a
Stuhl und zur	new one on Rebus, who kept quiet. 'I'd like a present.'
Sache kam •	'Not just a card this year then?'
steht vor der Tür	'What I want, John, is Topper Hamilton.'
	Rebus let that sink in. 'I thought Topper was Mr Clean these days?'
für mich •	'Not in my books.' The Farmer cupped his hands
er hat sich	around his coffee mug. 'He got a fright last time and,
zurückgehalten	granted, he's been keeping a low profile, but we both
• Verbrecher	know the best villains have got little or no profile at all.'

Übung 6   Die folgenden Sätze enthalten jeweils einen grammatischen Fehler. Suchen und korrigieren Sie ihn.

1. Rebus's boss put his head over the door.
2. The Farmer were pouring a mug of coffee.
3. The Farmer offered Rebus some coffee, but he turned up the offer.
4. The Farmer told Rebus that it will soon be his birthday.
5. Rebus's boss folded the arms.

'So what's he been up to?'

'I heard a story he's the sleeping partner in a couple of clubs and casinos. I also hear he bought a taxi firm from Big Ger Cafferty when Big Ger went into Barlinnie.'

Rebus was thinking back three years to their big push against Topper Hamilton: they'd set up surveillance, used a bit of pressure here and there, got a few people to talk. In the end, it hadn't so much amounted to a hill of beans as to a fart in an empty can. The procurator fiscal had decided not to proceed to trial. But then God or Fate, call it what you like, had provided a spin to the story. Not a plague of boils or anything for Topper Hamilton, but a nasty little cancer which had given him more grief than the whole of the Lothian and Borders Police. He'd been in and out of hospital, endured chemo and the whole works, and had emerged a more slender figure in every sense.

The Farmer – who'd once settled an office argument by reeling off the books in both Old and New Testaments – wasn't yet content that God and life had done their worst to Topper, or that retribution had been meted out in some mysterious divine way. He

gemacht •
stiller Teilhaber

(Gefängnis in
Glasgow)

Überwachung •
war es nicht
wirklich überwältigend • Furz •
Staatsanwalt •
gerichtlich vorzugehen • Eiterbeulenpest • ihm
… Kummer bereitet hatte •
Chemotherapie
• der ganze
Krempel • herunterrasselte •
Strafe • zugemessen worden
war

Finden Sie die Wörter oder Sätze im Text, die das gleiche bedeuten wie die folgenden Begriffe.   **Übung 7**

1. remembering
2. to go to court
3. thinner
4. solved a dispute
5. was still not satisfied

schieben	wanted Topper in court, even if they had to wheel him there on a trolley. It was a personal thing.
soweit ich weiß	'Last time I looked,' Rebus said now, 'it wasn't illegal to invest in a casino.'
Überprüfung •	'It is if your name hasn't come up during the vetting procedure. Think Topper could get a gaming licence?'
Glücksspieler-	
laubnis • Stimmt.	'Fair point. But I still don't see –'
• Polizeispitzel	'Something else I heard. You've got a snitch works as a croupier.'
	'So?'
mit dem … zu	'Same casino Topper has a finger in.'
tun hat	Rebus saw it all and started shaking his head. 'I made him a promise. He'll tell me about punters, but nothing on the management.'
	'And you'd rather keep that promise than give me a birthday present?'
das ist ein Eier-	'A relationship like that … it's eggshells.'
tanz •	The Farmer's eyes narrowed. 'You think ours isn't? Talk to him, John. Get him to do some ferreting.'
herumzuschnüf-	
feln •	'I could lose a good snitch.'
Maulhelden	'Plenty more bigmouths out there.' The Farmer watched Rebus get to his feet. 'I was looking for you earlier. You were in the video room.'

Übung 8   Vervollständigen Sie die Sätze mit den folgenden Wörtern.
(management, court, croupier, invest, promise, come up)

1. The Farmer wants to get Topper in _____.

2. It isn't against the law to _____ in a casino.

3. Topper's name didn't _____ during the vetting procedure.

4. Rebus's snitch works as a _____.

5. Rebus made his snitch a _____.

6. Rebus's snitch won't give him information on the _____.

'A missing person.'

'Suspicious?'

Ein Vermisster.

Rebus shrugged. 'Could be. He went up to the bar for a round of drinks, never came back.'

zuckte mit den Schultern

'We've all done that in our time.'

'His parents are worried.'

'How old is he?'

'Twenty-three.'

The Farmer thought about it. 'Then what's the problem?'

Two

The problem was the past. A week before, he'd received a phone call from a ghost.

'Inspector John Rebus, please.'

'Speaking.'

Kommissar •
Am Apparat.

'Oh, hello there. You probably won't remember me.' A short laugh. 'That used to be a bit of a joke at school.'

Rebus, immune to every kind of phone call, had this pegged a crank. 'Why's that?' he asked, wondering which punchline he was walking into.

hatte ihn als Spinner abge-stempelt •
Pointe

'Because it's my name: Mee.' The caller spelt it for him. 'Brian Mee.'

Verwandeln Sie die direkte Rede im Text von „Suspicious?" bis „Then what's the problem?" in die indirekte Rede.

Übung 9

Beachten Sie: Alle Verben, die in der direkten Rede im Präsens bzw. im Perfekt oder Imperfekt stehen, werden in der indirekten Rede im Imperfekt bzw. Plusquamperfekt wiedergegeben. Modalverben wie will, can, may und shall werden in der indirekten Rede zu would, could, might und should. Und would, could, might und should in der direkten Rede ändern sich in der indirekten Rede nicht.

Beginnen Sie so: The Farmer asked if this was suspicious.

Inside Rebus's head, a fuzzy photograph took sudden shape – a mouth full of prominent teeth, freckled nose and cheeks, a kitchen-stool haircut. 'Barney Mee?' he said.

unscharf •
vorstehend •
von der Mutter
geschnittene
Haare • ja

More laughter on the line. 'Aye, they used to call me Barney. I'm not sure I ever knew why.'

Rebus could have told him: after Barney Rubble in *The Flintstones*. He could have added, because you were a dense wee bastard. But instead he asked how this ghost from his past was doing.

Familie
Feuerstein •
begriffsstutziges
kleines Arschloch

'No' bad, no' bad.' The laugh again; Rebus recognised it now as a sign of nerves.

• nicht schlecht

'So what can I do for you, Brian?'

'Well, me and Janis, we thought … Well, it was my mum's idea actually. She knew your dad. Both my mum and dad knew him, only my dad passed away, like. They all used to drink at the Goth.'

ist entschlafen

'Are you still in Bowhill?'

'Never quite escaped. Ach, it's all right really. I work in Glenrothes though. Lucky to have a job these days, eh? Mind, you've done well for yourself, Johnny. Do you still get called that?'

allerdings

'I prefer John.'

'I remember you hated it when anyone called you Jock.' Another wheezing laugh. The photo was even sharper now, bordered with a white edge the way photos always were in the past. A decent footballer, a bit of a terrier, the hair reddish-brown. Dragging his satchel along the ground until the stitching rubbed away. Always with some huge hard sweet in his mouth, crunching down on it, his nose running. And one incident: he'd lifted some nude mags from under his dad's side of the bed and brought them to the toilets next to the Miners' Institute, there to be pored over like textbooks. Afterwards, half a dozen twelve-year-old boys had looked at each other, minds fizzing with questions. 'So what can I do for you, Brian?'

keuchend

Schulranzen •
Naht

geklaut • Nackt-
magazine •
Freizeitzentrum
für Bergleute •
eifrig studiert •
Lehrbücher

'Like I say, it was my mum's idea. Only, she remembered you were in the police in Edinburgh – saw your name in the paper a while back – and she thought you could maybe help.'

'With what?'

'Our son. I mean, mine and Janis's. He's called Damon.'

'What's he done?' Rebus thought: something minor, and way outside his territory anyway.

etwas Kleines •
weit außerhalb

Auf welches Wort oder welchen Satz im Text beziehen sich die folgenden Erklärungen?

Übung 10

1. a small but very tough person
2. to crush something noisily between your teeth
3. a printed work which teaches about a particular subject
4. to become excited and full of energy
5. of limited importance
6. area

'He's vanished.'

'Run away?'

Eher wie vom Erdboden verschluckt. •
Freunde • hielt inne • Polizei •
abweisend • schnüffelten ... herum • abzuhauen

'More like in a puff of smoke. He was in this club with his pals, see, and he went –'

'Have you tried calling the police?' Rebus caught himself. 'I mean Fife Constabulary.'

'Oh aye.' Mee sounded dismissive. 'They asked a few questions, like, sniffed around a bit, then said there was nothing they could do. Damon's twenty-three. They say he's got a right to bugger off if he wants.'

'They've got a point. People run away all the time, Brian. Girl trouble maybe.'

verlobt

'He was engaged.'

'Maybe he got scared?'

lautes Wort

'Helen's a lovely girl. Never a raised voice between them.'

'Did he leave a note?'

'Nothing. I went through this with the police. He didn't take any clothes or anything. He didn't have any reason to go.'

'So you think something's happened to him?'

Arschlöcher

'I know what those buggers are thinking. They say we should give him another week or so to come back, or at

---

Übung 11   Beantworten Sie die Fragen zum Text. Welche Lösung ist die richtige?

1. How did the Fife police react when Brian contacted them?
   a) They arrested him for his son's murder.
   b) They made a few enquiries.
   c) They told him to phone Rebus.

2. What was Brian's son's relationship with his girlfriend like?
   a) They never argued.
   b) They hated one another.
   c) He didn't have a girlfriend.

least get in touch but I know they'll only start doing something about it when the body turns up.'

sich zu melden

Again, Rebus could have confirmed that this was only sensible. Again, he knew Mee wouldn't want to hear it. 'The thing is, Brian,' he said, 'I work in Edinburgh. Fife's not my patch. I mean, I can make a couple of phone calls, but it's hard to know what else to do.'

Revier

The voice was close to despair. 'Well, if you could just do *some*thing. Like, anything. We'd be very grateful. It would put our minds at rest.' A pause. 'My mum always speaks well of your dad. He's remembered in this town.' And buried there, too, Rebus thought. He picked up a pen. 'Give me your phone number, Brian.' And, almost an afterthought, 'Better give me the address, too.'

Verzweiflung

uns beruhigen

nachträglicher Einfall

That evening, he drove north out of Edinburgh, paid his toll at the Forth Bridge, and crossed into Fife. It wasn't as if he never went there – he had a brother in Kirkcaldy. But though they spoke on the phone every month or so, there were seldom visits. He couldn't think of any other family he still had in Fife. The place liked to call itself 'the Kingdom' and there were those who would agree that it was another country, a place

Mautgebühr

3. When will the Fife police take action, according to Brian?
   a) In a month's time.
   b) When Damon phones them.
   c) When Damon's body is found.

4. Which members of Rebus's family live in Fife?
   a) His mother and father.
   b) His brother.
   c) He has no family in Fife.

Währung •
kompliziert

Fremde •
Küstenlandschaft

Werften

vorsichtig •
nach innen
gewandt •
Wahrzeichen
• gut dreißig
Jahre • Zeit-
spanne

anders als

with its own linguistic and cultural currency. For such a small place it seemed almost endlessly complex – had seemed that way to Rebus even when he was growing up. To outsiders the place meant coastal scenery and St Andrew's, or a stretch of motorway between Edinburgh and Dundee, but the west-central Fife of Rebus's childhood had been very different, ruled by coal mines and linoleum, dockyards and chemical plants, an industrial landscape shaped by basic needs, and producing people who were wary and inward-looking with the blackest humour you'd ever find.

They'd built new roads since Rebus's last visit, and knocked down a few more landmarks, but the place didn't feel so very different from thirty-odd years before. It wasn't such a great span of time after all, except in human terms; maybe not even then. Entering Cardenden – Bowhill had disappeared from road signs in the 1960s, even if locals still knew it as a village distinct from its neighbour – Rebus slowed to see if the memories would turn out sweet or sour. Then he caught sight of a Chinese takeaway and thought: both, of course. Brian and Janis Mee's house was easy enough to find: they were standing by the gate waiting

Übung 12 Setzen Sie die Verben in die in Klammern angegebene Zeitform.

1. To outsiders the place meant coastal scenery. (Präsens)
2. The west-central Fife of Rebus's childhood had been very different. (Imperfekt)
3. They'd built new roads. (Verlaufsform der Gegenwart)
4. The place didn't feel so very different. (Futur)
5. Locals still knew it as a village distinct from its neighbour. (Präsens)

for him. Rebus had been born in a prefab but brought up in a house just like the one he now parked in front of. Brian Mee practically opened the car door for him, and was trying to shake his hand while Rebus was still emerging from his seat.

'Let the man catch his breath!' Janis Mee snapped. She was still standing by the gate, arms folded. 'How have you been, Johnny?'

And Rebus realised that Brian Mee had married Janis Playfair, the only girl in his long and trouble-strewn life who'd ever managed to knock him unconscious.

The narrow, low-ceilinged living-room was full to bursting – not just Rebus and Janis and Brian, but Brian's mother and Mr and Mrs Playfair. Introductions had to be made, and Rebus guided to 'the seat by the fire'. The room was overheated. A pot of tea was produced, and on the table by Rebus's armchair sat enough slices of cake to feed a football crowd.

'He's a brainy one,' Janis's mother said, handing Rebus a framed photo of Damon Mee. 'Plenty of certificates from school. Works hard. Saving up to get married. The date's set for next August.'

Margin glosses:
- Fertighaus
- noch ausstieg
- schnauzte
- voller Schwierigkeiten • ihn k.o. zu schlagen •
- mit einer tief sitzenden Decke
- gescheit

Die folgenden Sätze enthalten jeweils einen grammatischen Fehler. Suchen und korrigieren Sie ihn.   **Übung 13**

1. Rebus had been brought round in a similar house to Brian's.
2. Brian practical opened the car door for Rebus.
3. Brian was trying to shake the hand while Rebus was still emerging from his seat.
4. Rebus was guided to the seat on the fire.
5. Janis tells Rebus that Damon is saving up to become married.
6. The date of the wedding is set on next August.

Lausbub •
etwas Neueres

The photo showed a smiling imp, not long out of school. 'Have you got anything more recent?'

Janis handed him a packet of snapshots. 'From last summer.'

es ersparte ihm

Heilmittel

schelmisch •
vergrämt •
Desillusionierung
• Erwachsensein

Rebus went through them slowly. It saved having to look at the faces around him. He felt like a doctor, expected to produce an immediate diagnosis and remedy. The photos showed a man in his early twenties, still retaining the impish smile but recognisably older. Not careworn exactly, but with something behind the eyes, some disenchantment with adulthood. A few of the photos showed Damon's parents.

'We all went together,' Brian explained. 'Janis's mum and dad, my mum, Helen and her parents.'

Beaches, a big white hotel, poolside games. 'Where is it?'

'Lanzarote,' Janis said, handing him his tea. In a few of the pictures she was wearing a bikini – good body for her age, or any age come to that. He tried not to linger.

eigentlich •
nicht länger bei
dem Gedanken
zu verweilen

'Can I keep a couple of the close-ups?' he asked. Janis looked at him. 'Of Damon.' She nodded and he put the other photos back in their packet.

'We're really grateful,' someone said. Janis's mum? Brian's? Rebus couldn't tell.

Übung 14

Sind die folgenden Aussagen wahr oder falsch?
Tragen Sie ein T für true oder ein F für false in die Kästchen ein.

1. The first photo Rebus sees shows Damon just after he left school.
2. Rebus is glad not to have to look at the faces of the people around him.
3. Damon spent his holiday in Lanzarote alone with his parents.
4. Rebus thinks Janice looks attractive in her bikini.
5. Rebus wants to keep a couple of the photos of Damon.

'Does Helen live locally?' am Ort

'Practically round the corner.'

'I'd like to talk to her.'

'I'll give her a bell,' Brian Mee said, leaping to his feet. rufe sie an •

'Damon had been drinking in some club?' und sprang auf

'Guisers,' Janis said, handing round cigarettes. 'It's in Kirkcaldy.'

'On the Prom?' Strandprome-

She shook her head, looking just the same as she had nade
that night of the school dance ... shaking her head,
telling him so far and no further. 'In the town. It used
to be a department store.'

'It's really called Gaitanos,' Mr Playfair said. Rebus
remembered him, too. He was an old man now.

'Where does Damon work?' Careful to stick to the present tense. Brian Mee came back into the room. 'Same
place I do. I managed to get him a job in packaging. He's
been learning the ropes; it'll be management soon.' hat sich eingear-

Working-class nepotism; jobs handed down from beitet • Vettern-
father to son. Rebus was surprised it still existed. wirtschaft •
                                                         weitergegeben
'Helen'll be here in a minute,' Brian added.

'Are you not eating any cake, Inspector?' said Mrs Playfair.

6. Helen lives on the far side of town.

7. Mr Playfair volunteers to phone Helen.

8. Guisers overlooks the beach in Kirkcaldy.

9. The building in which Guisers is located has always
   been a night club.

10. Damon and his father work for the same company.

11. Damon's father used his influence to get a job for his son.

12. Mrs Playfair is angry because Rebus has eaten all the cake.

Helen Cousins hadn't been able to add much to Rebus's picture of Damon, and hadn't been there the night he'd vanished. But she'd introduced him to someone who had, Andy Peters. Andy had been part of the group at Gaitanos. There'd been four of them. They'd been in the same year at school and still met up once or twice a week, sometimes to watch Raith Rovers* if the weather was decent and the mood took them, other times for an evening session in a pub or club. It was only their third or fourth visit to Guisers.

Rebus thought of paying the club a visit, but knew he should talk to the local cops first, and decided that it could all wait until morning. He knew he was jumping through hoops. He didn't expect to find anything the locals had missed. At best, he could reassure the family that everything possible had been done.

Next morning he made a few phone calls from his office, trying to find someone who could be bothered to answer some casual questions from an Edinburgh colleague. He had one ally – Detective Sergeant Hendry at Dunfermline CID – but only reached him at the third attempt. He asked Hendry for a favour, then

---

Marginal notes (left column):

sie stellte ihm … vor

wenn sie dazu aufgelegt waren • Abend

dass das alles nur Schaulaufen war • Leute vor Ort • versichern

den Nerv hatte • beiläufig • Polizeimeister • Kriminalpolizei

---

info   Die Raith Rovers sind ein schottischer Fußballverein in Kirkcaldy.

Übung 15   Wie viele Verben stehen in den ersten fünf Zeilen auf dieser Seite im Plusquamperfekt, also der Vorvergangenheit? Schreiben Sie die Zeilen ab und setzen Sie die Verben dabei ins Imperfekt.

put the phone down and got back to his own work. But it was hard to concentrate. He kept thinking about Bowhill and about Janis Mee, nee Playfair. Which led him – eventually – guiltily – to thoughts of Damon. Younger runaways tended to take the same route: by bus or train or hitching, and to London, Newcastle, Edinburgh or Glasgow. There were organisations who would keep an eye open for runaways, and even if they wouldn't always reveal their whereabouts to the anxious families, at least they could confirm that someone was alive and unharmed.

geborene •
schließlich •
Ausreißer •
per Anhalter

Ausschau halten nach • Verbleib

But a twenty-three-year-old, someone a bit cannier and with money to hand ... could be anywhere. No destination was too distant – he owned a passport, and it hadn't turned up. Rebus knew, too, that Damon had a current account at the local bank, complete with cash-card, and an interest-bearing account with a building society* in Kirkcaldy. The bank might be worth trying. Rebus picked up the telephone again.

schlauer •
Reiseziel

Girokonto •
Geldautomaten-
karte • Sparkonto
• Bausparkasse •

The manager at first insisted that he'd need something in writing, but relented when Rebus promised to fax him later. Rebus held while the manager went off to check, and had doodled half a village, complete with

Filialleiter •
er gab nach •
blieb am Apparat
• gekritzelt

info

In den letzten zwanzig Jahren sind die Unterschiede zwischen Banken und Bausparkassen in Großbritannien fast verschwunden. Früher waren die meisten Bausparkassen Gesellschaften auf genossenschaftlicher Grundlage. Heutzutage aber sind fast alle Aktiengesellschaften wie die Banken. Girokonten, Sparkonten und Geldkarten gibt es wie in Deutschland, aber in Großbritannien ist es viel üblicher, ein Scheckbuch für das persönliche Girokonto zu haben. Bankkarten (debit cards) und Kreditkarten sind auch sehr beliebt, und in Großbritannien ist es normal, die monatliche Abrechnung einer Kreditkarte in Raten abzuzahlen.

stream, parkland and school, by the time the man came back.

Abhebung •
Geldautomat

'The most recent withdrawal was from a cash machine in Kirkcaldy. One hundred pounds on the twenty-second.'

'What time?'

'I've no way of knowing.'

'No other withdrawals since then?'

'No.'

aktuell •

'How up-to-date is that information?'

vordatiert

'Very. Of course a cheque – especially if post-dated – would take longer to show up.'

ein wachsames
Auge auf …
haben •

'Could you keep tabs on that account, let me know if anyone starts using it again?'

eine Genehmi-
gung der Haupt-
geschäftsstelle

'I could, but I'd need it in writing, and I might also need Head Office approval.'

'Well, see what you can do, Mr Brayne.'

'It's Bain,' the bank manager said coldly, putting down the phone.

rief ihn erst …
zurück •
zwielichtig

DS Hendry didn't get back to him until late afternoon.

'Gaitanos,' Hendry said. 'I don't know the place personally. Locals call it Guisers. It's a pretty choice establishment. Two stabbings last year, one inside the club

Übung 16   Die folgende Zusammenfassung des Textes auf dieser Seite enthält drei sachliche Fehler. Können Sie sie finden und korrigieren?

The bank teller tells Rebus that Damon withdrew one hundred pounds from his account in Kirkcaldy on the twenty-second but that he did not know the exact time of the transaction. The information is not very up-to-date, however. Rebus asks the manager to keep an eye on the account and let him know if anyone uses it again. The manager can see no reason why he shouldn't do this. Later Rebus receives a call from DS Hendry about the Gaitanos club.

itself, the other in the back alley where the owner parks his Merc. Local residents are always girning about the noise when the place lets out.'

meckern • zumacht

'What's the owner's name?'

'Charles Mackenzie, nicknamed "Charmer". He seems to be clean. A couple of uniforms talked to him about Damon Mee, but there was nothing to tell. Know how many missing persons there are every year? They're not exactly a white-hot priority. God knows there are times I've felt like doing a runner myself.'

uniformierte Polizisten • Vermisste • höchste Priorität • abzuhauen •

'Haven't we all? Did the woolly suits talk to anyone else at the club?'

uniformierte Polizisten •

'Such as?'

'Bar staff, punters.'

zum Beispiel • Barpersonal

'No. Someone did take a look at the security video for the night Damon was there, but they didn't see anything.'

'Where's the video now?'

'Back with its rightful owner.'

'Am I going to be stepping on toes if I ask to see it?'

jemandem auf den Schlips treten • decken

'I think I can cover you. I know you said this was personal, John, but why the interest?'

'I'm not sure I can explain.' There were words –

Auf welches Wort oder welchen Satz im Text beziehen sich die folgenden Erklärungen?

Übung 17

1. a narrow lane behind or between buildings

2. a person who lives in a particular place

3. not having done anything illegal

4. something which should be dealt with first

5. correct or legal

Gemeinschaft

community, history, memory – but Rebus didn't think they'd be enough.

'They mustn't be working you hard enough over there.'

'Just the twenty-four hours every day.'

Three

Kreuzfahrtschiffe

und gab … aus

Magnate

eingestellt • auf
dem Höhepunkt
• Trümmer
• von Hand-
feuerwaffen •
im Schein einiger
Taschenlampen
• Mangel an

Matty Paine could tell a few stories. He'd worked his way round the world as a croupier. Cruise liners he'd worked on, and in Nevada. He'd spent a couple of years in London, dealing out cards and spinning the wheel for some of the wealthiest in the land, faces you'd recognise from the TV and the papers. Moguls, royalty, stars – Matty had seen them all. But his best story – the one people sometimes disbelieved – was about the time he'd been recruited to work in a casino in Beirut. This was at the height of the civil war, bomb sites and rubble, smoke and charred buildings, refugees and regular bursts of small-arms fire. And amazingly, in the midst of it all (or, to be fair, on the edge of it all), a casino. Not exactly legal. Run from a hotel basement with torchlight when the generator failed and not much in the way of refreshments, but with no shortage of pun-

Übung 18

Das Wort „wealthiest" (am reichsten) ist der Superlativ, also die Steigerung, des Adjektivs „wealthy" (reich). Setzen Sie die folgenden Adjektive wie im Beispiel in den Komparativ und den Superlativ. Aber passen Sie auf! Einige sind unregelmäßig.
Beispiel: cold, colder, coldest

brave	tiny
good	horrible
boring	cheap
hot	bad

ters – cash bets, dollars only – and a management team of three who prowled the place like Dobermanns, since there was no surveillance and no other way to check that the games were being played honestly. One of them had stood next to Matty for a full forty minutes one session, making him sweat despite the air-conditioning. He'd reminded Matty of the gaffers casinos employed to check on apprentices. He knew the gaffers were there to protect *him* as much as the punters – there were professional gamblers out there who'd psych out a trainee, watch them for hours, whole nights and weeks, looking for the flaw that would give them an edge over the house. Like, when you were starting out, you didn't always vary the force with which you span the wheel, or sent the ball rolling, and if they could suss it, they'd get a pretty good idea which quadrant the ball was going to stop in. Good croupiers were immune to this. A really good croupier – one of a very select, very highly thought of group – could master the wheel and get the ball to land pretty well where *they* wanted.

Of course, this might be against the interests of the house, too. And in the end, that's why the checkers

herumschlichen

Vorarbeiter •
um … zu kon-
trollieren • Lehr-
linge • Glücks-
spieler •
erkennen • Fehler
• Vorteil •
Anfänger war

dahinterkommen

hochgeschätzt

Haus (Firma)

Ordnen Sie den folgenden Wörtern aus dem Text die passende deutsche Übersetzung zu.

bet	beherrschen
surveillance	Fehler
trainee	erlesen
flaw	ändern
vary	Wette
select	Auszubildender
master	Überwachung

were out there, patrolling the tables. They were looking out for the house. In the end it all came down to the house. And when things had got a wee bit too hot in London, Matty had come home, meaning Edinburgh, though really he was from Gullane – perhaps the only boy ever to be raised there and not show the slightest interest in golf*. His father had played – his mother too, come to that. Maybe she still did; he didn't keep in touch. There had been an awkward moment at the casino when a neighbour from Gullane days, an old business friend of his father's, had turned up, a bit the worse for wear and in tow with three other middle-aged punters. The neighbour had glanced towards Matty from time to time, but had eventually shaken his head, unable to place the face.

'Does he know you?' one of the all-seeing gaffers had asked quietly, seeking out some scam against the house.

Matty had shaken his head. 'A neighbour from when I was growing up.' That was all; just a ghost from the past. He supposed his mother *was* still alive. He could probably find out by opening the phone book. But he wasn't that interested.

Margin glosses:

kam es alles auf … an

aufgezogen wurde

heikel

angetrunken • zusammen mit • hatte flüchtig auf … geblickt • herauszufinden, woher er ihn kannte • betrügerische Masche

info

Zusammen mit Fußball ist Golf eine nationale Leidenschaft in Schottland. Das Spiel wurde dort im sechzehnten Jahrhundert erfunden, und der älteste Golfplatz der Welt befindet sich in St. Andrews an der Ostküste, einer Stadt, die als Heimat des Golfsports gilt. Dort wurde 1754 auch einer der ersten Golfklubs gegründet. Das Ziel des Spiels ist, einen Ball mit möglichst wenigen Schlägen in ein Loch zu spielen. Dabei kommen verschiedene Golfschläger zum Einsatz. Eine Runde Golf besteht aus 18 Spielbahnen, die nacheinander absolviert werden müssen.

'Place your bets, please, ladies and gentlemen.'

Different houses had different styles. You either did your spiel in English or French. House rules changed, too. Matty's strengths were roulette and blackjack, but really he was happy in charge of any sort of game – most houses liked that he was flexible, it meant there was less chance of him trying some scam. It was the one-note wonders who tried small, stupid diddles. His latest employers seemed fairly laid back. They ran a clean casino which boasted only the very occasional high roller. Most of the punters were business people, well enough heeled but canny with it. You got husbands and wives coming in, proof of a relaxed atmosphere. There were younger punters too – a lot of those were Asians, mainly Chinese. The money they changed, according to the cashier, had a funny feel and smell to it.

'That's because they keep it in their underwear,' the day boss had told her.

The Asians … whatever they were … sometimes worked in local restaurants; you could smell the kitchen on their crumpled jackets and shirts. Fierce gamblers, no game was ever played quickly enough for their liking.

Sprüche

für ... verant-
wortlich zu sein

Menschen, die
nur ein Talent
haben • Betrüge-
reien • gelassen
• Spieler, der um
hohe Einsätze
spielt • gut
genug betucht

zerknittert •
erbittert

Vervollständigen Sie die folgenden Sätze mit den angegebenen Wörtern. (laid-back, crumpled, Asian, flexible, relaxed atmosphere, underwear)

1. Most houses like the fact that Matty is _____.

2. Matty's latest employers seem _____.

3. Husbands and wives coming in is proof of a _____.

4. A lot of the younger punters are _____.

5. The day boss thinks the Asians keep their money
 in their _____.

6. The Asians wear _____ jackets and shirts.

ihre Spielmarken	They'd slap their chips down like they were in a play-
hinschmeißen	ground betting game. And they talked a lot, almost
	never in English. The gaffers didn't like that, never
ausheckten	could tell what they might be scheming. But their
	money was good, they seldom caused trouble, and they
Anteil •	lost a percentage same as everyone else.
blöd •	'Daft bastards,' the night manager said. 'Know what
Sie setzen es	they do with a big win? Go bung it on the gee-gees.
auf Pferde. •	Where's the sense in that?'
Buchmacher	Where indeed? No point giving your money to a book-
	maker when the casino would happily take it instead.
es war eigentlich	It wasn't really on for croupiers to be friends with the
nicht akzeptabel	clients, but sometimes it happened. And it couldn't
	very well not happen with Matty and Stevie Scoular,
	since they'd been in the same year at school. Not that
	they'd known one another well. Stevie had been the
recht gut	football genius, also more than fair at the hundred and
	two hundred metres, swimming and basketball. Matty,
geschwänzt •	on the other hand, had skived off games whenever pos-
Sport • Sachen	sible, forgetting to bring his kit or getting his mum to
• Entschuldi-	write him notes. He was good at a couple of subjects –
gungen •	maths and woodwork – but never sat beside Stevie in
Tischlerei	class. They even lived at opposite ends of the town.

Übung 21 Ersetzen Sie alle Substantive und Namen in den folgenden Sätzen durch die entsprechenden Personalpronomen.

Beispiel: The gamblers seldom trouble the manager.
  They seldom trouble him.

1. The mother wrote a note for Matty.
2. The night manager didn't approve of the Asians.
3. The casino is next door to the police station.
4. Rebus used to go out with Janis.
5. Janis is now married to Brian.

At playtime and lunchtime, Matty ran a card game – three-card brag mostly, sometimes pontoon – playing for dinner money*, pocket money, sweets and comics. A few of the cards were nicked at the corners, but the other players didn't seem to notice and Matty got a reputation as 'lucky'. He'd take bets on horse races too, sometimes passing the bets on to an older boy who wouldn't be turned away by the local bookmaker. Often though, Matty would simply pocket the money and if someone's horse happened to win, he'd say he couldn't get the bets on in time and hand back the stake.

He couldn't tell you exactly when it was that Stevie had started spending less breaktime dribbling past half a dozen despairing pairs of legs and more hanging around the edges of the card school. Thing about three-card brag, it doesn't take long to pick it up and even a moron can have a stab at playing. Soon enough, Stevie was losing his dinner money with the rest of them, and Matty's pockets were about bursting with loose change. Eventually, Stevie had seemed to see sense, drifted away from the game and back to keepie-up and dribbling. But he'd been hooked, no doubt about it. Maybe only for a few weeks, but a lot of

organisierte •
(Kartenspiel) •
17 und 4 •
eingekerbt

fortgeschickt
werden • in die
eigene Tasche
stecken • Einsatz

Pause

um es zu lernen
• Schwachkopf
• versuchen zu
spielen

Ball-Jonglieren
• es hatte ihn
erwischt

Da der Schultag in Großbritannien erst zwischen drei und vier Uhr nachmittags endet, ist es üblich, in der Schule zu Mittag zu essen. Früher brachte man jeden Montag das Essensgeld für die ganze Woche mit zur Schule. Heutzutage gibt es für gewöhnlich eine Kantine, in der man jeden Tag für das Essen bezahlt. School dinners waren bislang oft von geringer Qualität und deshalb eine Zielscheibe des Spotts im ganzen Land. In den letzten paar Jahren aber hat sich diese Lage geändert. Jetzt verlangen immer mehr Eltern, dass ihre Kinder auch in der Schule gesund essen können.

info

those lunchtimes had been spent cadging sweets and apple cores, the better to stave off hunger.

Even then, Matty had thought he'd be seeing Stevie again. It had just taken the best part of a decade, that was all.

When Stevie Scoular walked into the casino, people looked his way. It was the done thing. He was a sharp dresser, young, usually accompanied by women who looked like models. When Stevie had first walked into the Morvena, Matty's heart had sunk. They hadn't seen one another since school and here Stevie was, local boy made good, a hero, picture in the papers and plenty of money in the bank. Here was a schoolboy dream made flesh. And what was Matty? He had stories he could tell but that was about it. So he'd been hoping Stevie wouldn't grace his table, or if he did that he wouldn't recognise him. But Stevie had seen him, seemed to know him straight off and come bouncing up.

'Matty!'

'Hello there, Stevie.'

It was flattering really. Stevie hadn't become big-headed or anything. He took the whole thing – the way his

Marginal notes

große Pausen •
zu schnorren •
um … zu lindern
• fast ein Jahr-
zehnt

Das war eben so
üblich. • er war
todschick ange-
zogen • hatte
Matty der Mut
verlassen •
erfolgreich •
der sich erfüllt
hatte • das war
alles • mit sei-
ner Anwesenheit
beehren • war
munter auf ihn
zugekommen

Übung 22

Welche der folgenden Adjektive beschreiben Stevie?

penniless
ugly
smartly-dressed
famous
ancient
arrogant
friendly

life had gone – as a bit of a joke really. He'd made Matty promise to meet him for a drink when his shift was over. All through their conversation, Matty had been aware of gaffers hovering and when Stevie wandered off to another table one of them muttered in Matty's ear and another croupier took over from him.

He hadn't been in the plush back office that often, just for the initial interview and to discuss a couple of big losses on his table. The casino's owner, Mr Mandelson, was watching a football match on Sky Sports. He was well-built, mid-forties, his face pockmarked from childhood acne. His hair was black, slicked back from the forehead, long at the collar. He always seemed to know what he was about.

'How's the table tonight?' he asked.

'Look, Mr Mandelson, I know we're not supposed to be too friendly with the punters, but Stevie and me were at school together. Haven't clapped eyes on one another since – not till tonight.'

'Easy, Matty, easy.' Mandelson motioned for him to sit down. 'Something to drink?' A smile. 'No alcohol on shift, mind.'

'Ehh … a Coke maybe.'

Schicht

die sich in der Nähe aufhielten • löste ihn ab • elegant • erst

kräftig • pocken-narbig • ge-schniegelt

nicht zu sehen gekriegt • immer mit der Ruhe

Welche der folgenden Adjektive beschreiben Herrn Mandelson?   **Übung 23**

bald
blond
young
dark-haired
middle-aged
puny
scarred

'Help yourself.'

gefüllt •

There was a fridge in the far corner, stocked with white

alkoholfreie

wine, champagne and soft drinks. A couple of the

Getränke • es

female croupiers said Mandelson had tried it on with

bei ihnen ver-

them, plying them with booze. But he didn't seem

sucht hatte •

upset by a refusal: they still had their jobs. There were

indem er sie

seven female croupiers all told, and only two had spo-

zum Trinken

ken to Matty about it. It made him wonder about the

genötigt hatte •

other five.

insgesamt

He took a Coke and sat down again.

'So, you and Stevie Scoular, eh?'

'I haven't seen him in here before.'

'I think he only recently found out about the place.

gewaltig

He's been in a few times, dropped some hefty bets.'
Mandelson was staring at him. 'You and Stevie, eh?'

'Look, if you're worried, just take me off whatever table
he's playing.'

'Nothing like that, Matty.' Mandelson's face broke into
a grin. 'It's nice to have a friend, eh? Nice to meet up
again after all these years. Don't you worry about anything. Stevie's the King of Edinburgh. As long as he

Untertanen

keeps scoring goals, we're all his subjects.' He paused.
'Nice to know someone who knows the King, almost

Übung 24   Beantworten Sie die Fragen zum Text. Welche Lösung ist die richtige?

1. What does the fridge in the corner contain?
   a) Some cheese and a loaf of bread.
   b) Some alcoholic and non-alcoholic drinks.
   c) Mr Mandelson's sandwiches.

2. How long will Stevie be 'King of Edinburgh'?
   a) Five years.
   b) Until the end of the summer.
   c) As long as he keeps scoring goals.

makes me feel like royalty myself. On you go now, Matty.'

du kannst jetzt gehen

Matty got up, leaving the Coke unopened.

'And don't you go upsetting that young man. We don't want to put him off his game, do we?'

wir wollen ihm nicht das Spiel verderben

Four

It had taken a couple of days to get the tape from Gaitanos. At first, they thought they'd wiped it, and then they'd sent the wrong day's recording. But at last Rebus had the right tape and had watched it at home half a dozen times before deciding he could use someone who knew what he was doing ... and a video machine that would freeze-frame without the screen looking like a technical problem.

gelöscht

anhalten

Now he'd seen all there was to see. He'd watched a young man cease to exist. Of course, Hendry was right, a lot of people disappeared every year. Sometimes they turned up again – dead or alive – and sometimes they didn't. What did it have to do with Rebus, beyond the promise to a family that he'd make sure the Fife police hadn't missed something? Maybe the pull wasn't Damon Mee, but Bowhill itself; and maybe even then,

der aufhörte

Anziehungskraft

3. How long does it take Rebus to get the video tape?
  a) A couple of days.
  b) A week.
  c) The video tape has been lost.

4. What does Rebus decide he needs after viewing the video?
  a) A pint of beer and a bag of crisps.
  b) A bath and a cup of hot chocolate.
  c) An expert on videos and a better video machine.

the Bowhill of his past rather than the town as it stood today.

He was working the Damon Mee case in his free time, which, since he was on day shift at St Leonard's, meant the evenings. He'd checked again with the bank – no money had been withdrawn from any machines since the twenty-second – and with Damon's building society. No money had been withdrawn from that account either. Even this wasn't unknown in the case of a runaway; sometimes they wanted to shed their whole history, which meant ditching their identity and everything that went with it. Rebus had passed a description of Damon to hostels and drop-in centres in Edinburgh, and faxed the same description to similar centres in Glasgow, Newcastle, Aberdeen and London. He'd also faxed details to the National Missing Persons Bureau in London. He checked with a colleague who knew about 'MisPers' that he'd done about all he could.

'Not far off it,' she confirmed. 'It's like looking for a needle in a haystack without knowing which field to start with.'

'How big a problem is it?'

She puffed out her cheeks. 'Last figures I saw were for

Margin glosses:
ablegen • wegzuschmeißen

Wohnheime und Treffpunkte für Obdachlose

Vermisste •

eine Nadel im Heuhaufen zu suchen

blies ... auf

Übung 25   Die folgenden Sätze enthalten jeweils einen grammatischen Fehler. Suchen und korrigieren Sie ihn.

1. Rebus was worked the case in his free time.
2. No money has been withdrawn out of the cash machine.
3. No money has been taken from those account.
4. Sometimes runaways want to shed the whole identity.
5. Rebus checks with a colleague that he had done all that he can.
6. The problem is like looking at a needle in a haystack.

the whole of Britain. I think there are around 25,000 a year. Those are the *reported* MisPers. You can add a few thousand for the ones nobody notices. There's a nice distinction actually: if nobody knows you're missing, are you really missing?'

Unterschied

Afterwards, Rebus telephoned Janis Mee and told her she might think about running up some flyers and putting them up in positions of prominence in nearby towns, maybe even handing them out to Saturday shoppers or evening drinkers in Kirkcaldy. A photo of Damon, a brief physical description, and what he was wearing the night he left. She said she'd already thought of doing so, but that it made his disappearance seem so final. Then she broke down and cried and John Rebus, thirty-odd miles away, asked if she wanted him to 'drop by'.

Flugblätter herzustellen • sie ... aufzuhängen • auffällig

brach ... zusammen • vorbeikommt

'I'll be all right,' she said.

'Sure?'

'Well ...'

Rebus reasoned that he was going to go to Fife anyway. He had to drop the tape back to Gaitanos, and wanted to see the club when it was lively. He'd take the photos

argumentierte • das Video bei ... vorbeibringen

Die folgende Zusammenfassung des Textes auf dieser Seite enthält drei sachliche Fehler. Können Sie sie finden und korrigieren?

Übung 26

Rebus's colleague tells him that there are approximately 25,000 missing persons a year which are not reported. Rebus then phones Janis and suggests to her that she might produce some flies which she could hang up around town and hand out to people. She should include a photo of Damon with a physical description of him and what he was wearing that night. When she starts crying, Rebus asks her if she'd like him to go away.

of Damon with him and show them around. He'd ask about the candyfloss blonde. The technician who had worked with the videotape had transferred a still to his computer and managed to boost the quality. Rebus had some hard copies in his pocket. Maybe other people who'd been queuing at the bar would remember something. Maybe.

übertragen •
Standbild •
erhöhen

His first stop, however, was the cemetery. He didn't have any flowers to put on his parents' grave, but he crouched beside it, fingers touching the grass. The inscription was simple, just names and dates really, and underneath, 'Not Dead, But at Rest in the Arms of the Lord'. He wasn't sure whose idea that had been, not his certainly. The headstone's carved lettering was inlaid with gold, but it had already faded from his mother's name. He touched the surface of the marble, expecting it to be cold, but finding a residual warmth there. A blackbird nearby was trying to worry food from the ground. Rebus wished it luck.

Friedhof

hockte •
Inschrift

Grabstein •
eingelegt • aus-
gebleicht •
zurückgeblieben
• zerren

By the time he reached Janis's, Brian was home from work. Rebus told them what he'd done so far, after which Brian nodded, apologised, and said he had a Burns Club* meeting. The two men shook hands.

---

info

Burns Clubs wurden in Schottland gegründet, um das Leben und die Werke des Nationaldichters Robert Burns zu würdigen. Burns (1759 – 1796) stammte aus der Grafschaft Ayrshire an der Südwestküste Schottlands und schrieb seine Gedichte in dem Dialekt dieser Gegend. Burns Clubs organisieren jedes Jahr eine Feier anlässlich der Burns Night (Robert Burns' Geburtstag am 25. Januar). Beim dann servierten Burns Supper ist es üblich, haggis, neeps and tatties (Haggis, also gefüllten Schafsmagen, Steckrüben- und Kartoffelpüree) zu essen, nachdem Burns' Gedicht To a Haggis verlesen wurde.

When the door closed, Janis and Rebus exchanged a
look and then a smile.

'I see that bruise finally faded,' she said.   blauer Fleck •

Rebus rubbed his right cheek. 'It was a hell of a punch.'   Schlag

'Funny how strong you can get when you're angry.'

'Sorry.'

She laughed. 'Bit late to apologise.'

'It was just …'

'It was everything,' she said. 'Summer holidays coming

up, all of us leaving school, you going off to join the   und dass du zum

army. The last school dance before all of that. That's   Militär gingst

what it was.' She paused. 'Do you know what happened

to Mitch?' She watched Rebus shake his head. 'Last I

heard,' she said, 'he was living somewhere down south.   im Süden •

The two of you used to be so close.'   eng befreundet

'Yes.'

She laughed again. 'Johnny, it was a long time ago,

don't look so solemn.' She paused. 'I've sometimes

wondered … ach, not for years, but just now and then I

used to wonder what would have happened … '

'If you hadn't punched me?'

She nodded. 'If we'd stayed together. Well, you can't   die Zeit zurück-

turn the clock back, eh?'   drehen

Finden Sie die Wörter oder Sätze im Text, die das gleiche bedeuten   **Übung 27**
wie die folgenden Begriffe.

1. swapped

2. blow

3. annoyed

4. to say sorry

5. vacation

6. serious

'Would the world be any better if we could?'

She stared at the window, not really seeing it. 'Damon would still be here,' she said quietly. A tear escaped her eye, and she fussed for a handkerchief in her pocket. Rebus got up and made towards her. Then the front door opened, and he retreated.

'My mum,' Janis smiled. 'She usually pops in around this time. It's like a railway station around here, hard to find any privacy.'

Then Mrs Playfair walked into the living-room.

'Hello, Inspector, thought that was your car. Is there any news?'

'I'm afraid not,' Rebus said. Janis got to her feet and hugged her mother, the crying starting afresh. 'There there, pet,' Mrs Playfair said quietly. 'There there.'

Rebus walked past the two of them without saying a word.

It was still early when he reached Gaitanos. He had a word with one of the bouncers, who was keeping warm in the lobby until things started getting busy, and the man lumbered off to fetch Charles Mackenzie, *aka* Charmer. It seemed strange to Rebus: here he was,

Margin glosses (left column):
suchte umständlich nach • näherte sich ihr •
kommt ... vorbei • ein Privatleben zu führen

stand auf • wieder • na komm, Schatz

Flur • trampelte davon • alias

Übung 28   Sind die folgenden Aussagen wahr oder falsch?
Tragen Sie ein T für true oder ein F für false in die Kästchen ein.

1. Rebus goes over to Janis when the front door opens.
2. People are constantly coming round to visit Janis and Brian.
3. Janis put her arms around her mother in greeting.
4. Rebus says goodbye as he leaves the two women.
5. Rebus speaks to one of the bouncers inside the nightclub.
6. The video camera is obviously not working.

standing in the very foyer he'd stared at for so long on the video monitor. The camera was high up in one corner with nothing to show whether it was working. Rebus gave it a wave anyway. If he disappeared tonight, it could be his farewell to the world. Abschied

'Inspector Rebus.' They'd spoken on the phone. The man who came forward to shake Rebus's hand stood about five feet four and was as thin as a cocktail glass. Rebus placed him in his mid-fifties. He wore a powder-blue suit and an open-necked white shirt with suntan and gold jewellery beneath. His hair was silver and thinning, but as well-cut as the suit. 'Come through to the office.'

war ca. 1,62 m groß •
schätzte, dass er Mitte fünfzig war
• taubenblau

Rebus followed Mackenzie down a carpeted corridor to a gloss-black door with a sign on it saying 'Private'. There was no door handle. Mackenzie unlocked the door and motioned for Rebus to go in.

mit Teppichbo-den • glänzend schwarz •
winkte Rebus hinein

'After you, sir,' Rebus said. You never knew what could be waiting behind a locked door.

What greeted Rebus this time was an office which seemed to double as a broom-cupboard. Mops and a vacuum cleaner rested against one wall. A bank of screens spread across three filing cabinets showed

auch als … zu dienen • Wand

7. Rebus and Charles Mackenzie have never spoken to one another before.

8. Mr Mackenzie is extremely short and thin and has greying hair.

9. Mr Mackenzie enters the office before Rebus.

10. The office also contains cleaning equipment.

what was happening inside and outside the club. Unlike the video Rebus had watched, these screens each showed a certain location.

'Are these recording?' Rebus asked. Mackenzie shook his head.

beweglich •
entdecken •
wie es sich ent-
wickelt • hat ...
schmutzig ge-
macht •
Zuschauer •
hob drohend
den Finger •
Schmirgelpapier

'We've got a roaming monitor, and that's the only recording we get. But this way, if we spot trouble anywhere, we can watch it unfold.'

'Like that knifing in the alley?'

'Messed up my Mercedes.'

'So I heard. Is that when you called the police? When your car stopped being a bystander?'

Mackenzie laughed and wagged a finger, but didn't answer. Rebus couldn't see where he'd earned his nickname. The guy had all the charm of sandpaper.

'I brought back your video.' Rebus placed it on the desk.

'All right to record over it now?'

computer-
verbessert

'I suppose so.' Rebus handed over the computer-enhanced photograph. 'The missing person is slightly right of centre, second row.'

Tussi

'Is that his doll?'

'Do you know her?'

Übung 29 Vervollständigen Sie die folgenden Sätze mit dem entsprechenden Possessivpronomen wie im Beispiel.

Beispiel: Rebus couldn't see where he'd earned (sein) nickname.
　　　　　 Rebus couldn't see where he'd earned his nickname.

1. I parked (mein) Mercedes in the alley.
2. Do you want (dein) video back?
3. We enhanced the photograph on (unser) computer.
4. Rebus is standing in (sein) office.
5. He is helping Janis and Brian to find (ihr) son.
6. Is that man (ihr) boyfriend?

'Wish I did.'

'You haven't seen her before.'

'She doesn't look the sort I'd forget.'

Rebus took back the picture. 'Mind if I show this around?'

'The place is practically empty.'

'I thought I might stick around.'   dableiben

Mackenzie frowned and studied the backs of his hands. 'Well, you know, it's not that I don't want to help or anything …'

'But?'

'Well, it's hardly conducive to a party atmosphere, is   einer Partystim-
it? That's our slogan – "The best party of your life, every   mung wenig
night!" – and I don't think a police officer mooching   förderlich • der
around asking questions is going to add to the ambi-   herumlungert
ence.'

'I quite understand, Mr Mackenzie. I was being thoughtless.' Mackenzie lifted his hands, palms towards Rebus: no problem, the hands were saying.

'And you're quite right,' Rebus continued. 'In fact, I'd
be a lot quicker if I had some assistance – say, a dozen   Hilfe
uniforms. That way, I wouldn't be "mooching around"
for nearly so long. In fact, let's make it a couple of

Ordnen Sie den folgenden Wörtern aus dem Text die passende
deutsche Übersetzung zu.

frown	Hilfe
continue	Handfläche
palm	Atmosphäre
thoughtless	die Stirn runzeln
assistance	fortfahren
ambience	rücksichtslos

der erste Fick
einer Jungfrau •

halt

Bündel
Zwanziger

finanzieller Anreiz
• Gebäude
• hauen Sie ab

der in der Fankur-
ve des Gegners
eingeschlossen ist
• dass es sich
schon herumge-
sprochen hatte •
Jungs

tolle Frau

dozen. We'll be in and out, quick as a virgin's first poke. Mind if I use your phone?'

'Whoah, wait a minute. Look, all I was saying was … Look, how much do you want?'

'Sorry, sir?'

Mackenzie reached into a desk drawer, lifted out a brick of twenties, pulled about five notes free. 'Will this do it?'

Rebus sat back. 'Am I to understand you're trying to offer me a cash incentive to leave the premises?'

'Whatever. Just slope off, eh?'

Rebus stood up. 'To me, Mr Mackenzie, that's an open invitation to stay.'

So he stayed. The looks he got from staff made him feel like a football fan trapped on the opposition's turf. The way they all shook their heads as soon as he held up the photo, he knew word had gone around. He had a little more luck with the punters. A couple of lads had seen the woman before.

'Last week, was it?' one asked the other. 'Maybe the week before.'

'Not long ago anyway,' the other agreed. 'Cracker, isn't she?'

Übung 31   Beantworten Sie die Fragen zum Text.

1. Where does Mr Mackenzie keep his money in his office?
2. How much money does Mr Mackenzie offer Rebus?
3. What effect does Mr Mackenzie's offer of money have on Rebus?
4. Do any of the staff at the club recognise the woman in the photo?
5. Who does recognise the woman in the photo?
6. What do the lads think about the woman in the photo?
7. How many times have the two men seen the woman in the photo at the club?

'Has she been in since?'

'Haven't seen her. Just that one night. Didn't quite get the nerve up to ask for a dance.'

hatte nicht den Mut

'Was she with anyone?'

'No idea.'

They didn't recognise Damon Mee though. They said they never paid much attention to blokes.

Typen •

'We're not that way inclined, sweetie.'

Das ist nicht unser Fall, Süßer. • so dass Rebus ein Gefühl der Übelkeit hatte • geneigt

The place was still only half full, but the bass was loud enough to make Rebus feel queasy. He managed to order an orange juice at the bar and just sat there, looking at the photo. The woman interested him. The way her head was angled, the way her mouth was open, she could have been saying something to Damon. A minute later, he was gone. Had she said she'd meet him somewhere? Had something happened at that meeting? He'd shown the photo to Damon's mates from that night. They remembered seeing her, but swore Damon hadn't introduced himself.

schworen

'She seemed sort of cold,' one of them had said. 'You know, like she wanted to be left alone.'

Rebus had studied the video again, watched her progress towards the bar, showing no apparent interest

offenkundig

8. Do they know if she was alone at the club?

9. Why don't they recognise Damon from the photo?

10. What effect does the bass have on Rebus?

11. Why does Rebus think the woman in the photo might have been speaking to Damon?

12. Did Damon's friends remember him talking to the woman in the photo?

in Damon's leaving. But then she'd turned and started pushing her way back through the ~~throng,~~ no drink to show for her long wait.

At midnight exactly, she'd left the nightclub. The final shot was of her turning left along the pavement, watched by a few people who were waiting to get in. And now Charles Mackenzie wanted to give Rebus money.

At three quid for an orange juice, maybe he should have taken it.

If the place had been heaving, maybe he wouldn't have noticed them. He was finishing his second drink and trying not to feel like a leper in a children's ward when he recognised one of the doormen. There was another man with him, tall and fat and pale. His idea of clubbing was probably the connection of baseball bat to skull. The bouncer was pointing Rebus out to him. Here we go, Rebus thought. They've brought in the professionals. The fat man said something to the bouncer, and they both retreated to the foyer, leaving Rebus with an empty glass and only one good reason to order another drink.

Marginal glossary (left column):

Menschenmenge • ohne einen Drink als Ergebnis der langen Warterei

Pfund

brechend voll • Aussätziger • Kinderstation • Türsteher • (Wortspiel: club = Knüppel, to go clubbing = in eine Disko gehen) • zeigte ihm Rebus • jetzt geht's los • zogen sich … zurück

---

Übung 32   Bilden Sie aus den folgenden Sätzen Bedingungssätze (if-Sätze) wie im Beispiel:

Beispiel: If the place is heaving, maybe he won't notice them.
If the place had been heaving, maybe he wouldn't have noticed them.

1. If Mr Mackenzie is not careful, Rebus will call for assistance.
2. If the woman in the photograph is a regular at the bar, someone will recognise her.
3. If Rebus takes the money, he will buy another orange juice.

Get it over with, he thought, sliding from his bar stool and walking around the dance floor. There was always the fire exit, but it led on to the alley and, if they were waiting for him there, the only witness would be Mackenzie's Mercedes. He wanted things kept as public as possible. The street outside would be busy, no shortage of onlookers and possible good Samaritans. Or at the very least, someone to call for an ambulance. He paused in the foyer and saw that the bouncer was back at his post on the front door. No sign of the fat man. Then he glanced along the corridor towards Mackenzie's office, and saw the fat man planted outside the door. He had his arms folded in front of him and wasn't going anywhere.

Rebus walked outside. The air had seldom tasted so good. He tried to calm himself with a few deep breaths. There was a car parked at the kerbside, a gold-coloured Rolls-Royce, with nobody in the driver's seat. Rebus wasn't the only one admiring the car, but he was probably alone in memorising its number plate.

He moved his own car to where he could see the Roller, then sat tight. Half an hour later, the fat man emerged, looking to left and right. He walked to the

Margin glossary: bringen wir's hinter uns • Barhocker • Tanzfläche • Notausgang • Zeuge • öffentlich • Zuschauer • barmherzige Samariter • Posten • Der Dicke war nirgendwo zu sehen.

am Randstein

der sich das Kennzeichen einprägte • Rolls-Royce • wartete

4. If Rebus leaves by the fire exit, someone will be waiting for him in the alley.

5. If Rebus is attacked on the street, someone will call an ambulance.

6. If Rebus tries to go back to Mr Mackenzie's office, the fat man will stop him.

7. If the other people admiring the car are more observant, they will memorise the number plate.

8. If the fat man is more careful, he will see Rebus in his car.

car, unlocked it and held open the back door. Only now did another figure emerge from the club. Rebus caught a swishing full-length black coat, sleek hair and chiselled face. The man slipped into the car, and the fat man closed the door and squeezed in behind the steering wheel.

wirbelnd •
bodenlang •
kantig • *zwängte sich*

Like them or not, you had to admire Rollers. They carried tonnage.

Five

Back in Edinburgh he parked his car and sat in it, smoking his eleventh cigarette of the day. He sometimes played this game with himself – I'll have one more tonight, and deduct one from tomorrow's allowance. Or he would argue that any cigarette after midnight came from the next day's stash. He'd lost count along the way, but reckoned by now he should be going whole days without a ciggie to balance the books. Well, when it came down to it, ten cigarettes a day or twelve, thirteen, fourteen – what difference did it make?

abziehen

Vorrat • *er hatte den Überblick verloren* •
Glimmstängel

The street he was parked on was quiet. Residential for the most part with big houses. There was a basement

Wohngebiet

Übung 33   Auf welches Wort oder welchen Satz im Text beziehen sich die folgenden Erklärungen?

1. to come out of an enclosed place
2. smooth and shiny
3. to leave a vehicle in a particular place for a period of time
4. to be or to keep equal in value to something else
5. room or rooms in a building below ground level
6. to consider something attractive or impressive

bar on the corner, but it did mostly lunchtime business from the offices on neighbouring streets. By ten, the place was usually locked up. Taxis rippled past him and the occasional drunk, hands in pockets, would weave slowly homewards. A few of the taxis stopped just in front of him and disgorged their fares, who would then climb half a dozen steps and push open the door to the Morvena Casino. Rebus had never been inside the place. He placed the occasional bet on the horses, but that was about it. Gave up doing the football pools*. He bought a National Lottery* ticket when opportunity arose, but often didn't get round to checking the numbers. He had half a dozen tickets lying around, any one of which could be his fortune. He quite liked the notion that he might have won a million and not know it; preferred it, in fact, to the idea of actually having the million in his bank account. What would he do with a million pounds? Same as he'd do with fifty thou – self-destruct. Only faster.

Janis had asked him about Mitch – Roy Mitchell, Rebus's best friend at school. The more time Rebus had spent with her, the less he'd seen of Mitch. They'd been going to join the army together, hoping they

trudelten • torkeln

spieen ihre Fahrgäste aus

Toto • Lotto • kam … nicht dazu

Idee

Riesen (=Tausend) • sich selbst zerstören

Während die meisten Länder in Europa schon seit langem eine Lotteriegesellschaft haben, ist das Lottospiel in Großbritannien etwas relativ Neues. Es wurde erst 1994 eingeführt. Vorher spielte fast jede Familie im Land allwöchentlich Toto (football pools), aber das neue Lotto hat diese Tradition bald ersetzt.
Das Hauptspiel ähnelt dem deutschen Lottospiel „6 aus 49", und die Ziehung findet, wie in Deutschland, jeden Mittwoch und Samstag statt. Wenn man nicht so lange warten will, hat man mit den Rubbelkarten (scratch cards) zu jeder Zeit die Chance, zu gewinnen.

sein Auge verlor

war losgezogen

• Urlaub

Schichtwechsel

bog nach links
ab • blinkte …
links • hupte •
fuhr den Wagen
zur Seite •
kurbelte das
Fenster herunter

wie gut er es …
hatte •
wohlhabend

might get the same regiment. Until Mitch lost his eye. That had been the end of that. The army hadn't wanted him any more. Rebus had headed off, sent Mitch a couple of letters, but by the time his first leave came, Mitch had already left Bowhill. Rebus had stopped writing after that … When the Morvena's door opened next, it was so eight or nine young people could leave. The shift changeover. Three of them turned one way, the rest another. Rebus watched the group of three. At the first set of lights, two kept going and one crossed the road and took a left. Rebus started his engine and followed. When the lights turned green, he signalled left and sounded his horn, then pulled the car over and wound down his window.

'Mr Rebus,' the young man said.

'Hello, Matty. Let's go for a drive.'

Officers from other cities, people Rebus met from time to time, would remark on how cushy he had it in Edinburgh. Such a beautiful place, and prosperous. So little crime. They thought to be dangerous a city had to look dangerous. London, Manchester, Liverpool – these places were dangerous in their eyes. Not Edinburgh,

Übung 34 Die folgende Zusammenfassung des Textes auf dieser Seite enthält drei sachliche Fehler. Können Sie sie finden und korrigieren?

Rebus's friend, Mitch, doesn't join the army because he injures his leg. At first, Rebus keeps in touch with him but after a while he stops writing.
The next time the casino door opens, seven or eight people leave. Three of them turn in one direction. Rebus follows one of them, pulls over, and invites Matty to come with him for a drink.
Many of Rebus's colleagues think he is lucky to work in Edinburgh.

not this sleepy walking-tour with its monuments and museums. Tourism aside, the lifeblood of the city was its commerce, and Edinburgh's commerce – banking, insurance and the like – was discreet. The city hid its secrets well, and its vices too. Potentially troublesome elements had been moved to the sprawling council estates which ringed the capital, and any crimes committed behind the thick stone walls of the city centre's tenements and houses were often muffled by those same walls. Which was why every good detective needed his contacts.

Rebus took them on a circuit – Canonmills to Ferry Road, back up to Comely Bank and through Stockbridge into the New Town again. And they talked.

'I know we had a sort of gentleman's agreement, Matty,' Rebus said.

'But I'm about to find out you're no gentleman?'

Rebus smiled. 'You're ahead of me.'

'I wondered how long it would take.' Matty paused, stared through the windscreen. 'You know I'll say no.'

'Will you?'

'I said at the start, no ratting on anyone I work with or work for. Just the punters.'

> Rundgang •
> außer • Lebens-
> ader • Handel •
> Bankwesen •
> und so weiter •
> diskret • Laster
> • schwierig •
> gemeindeeigene
> Wohnsiedlungen
> • Mietshäuser •
> gedämpft •
> Rundreise

> Verpfeifen von

Viele Verben werden im Englischen mit einer festen Präposition gebraucht, z. B. „to rat <u>on</u> someone". Setzen Sie in die folgenden Sätze die jeweils richtige Präposition ein.

Übung 35

1. The customer asked _____ a cup of coffee.
2. Her brother reminds me _____ my uncle.
3. The teacher asked us to write _____ our summer holidays.
4. Connor was looking _____ his football in the garden.
5. I can't stop thinking _____ you.
6. My sister doesn't agree _____ me.

gemolken

'Not even many of them. It's not like I've been milking you, Matty. I'll bet you've dozens of stories you haven't told me.'

'I work tables, Mr Rebus. People don't place a bet and then start yacking about some job they've pulled or some scam they're running.'

über irgendein Ding zu quasseln, das sie gedreht haben • Betrug • ange- heitert • nichts verheimlicht

'No, but they meet friends. They have a drink, get mellow. It's a relaxing place, so I've heard. And maybe then they talk.'

'I've not held anything back.'

'Matty, Matty.' Rebus shook his head. 'It's funny, I was just thinking tonight about that night we met. Do you remember?'

How could he forget? A couple of drinks after work, a car borrowed from a friend who was away on holiday. Matty hadn't been back long. Driving through the town was great, especially with a buzz on. Streets glistening after the rain. Late night, mostly taxis for company. He just drove and drove and, as the streets grew quieter, he pushed the accelerator a bit further, caught a string of green lights, then saw one turning red. He didn't know how good the tyres were, imagined braking hard and skidding in the wet. Fuck it, he put his foot down.

wenn man besoffen war • fast nur Taxis als Gesellschaft • gab ... Gas • zu schleudern • gab Gas

---

Übung 36

Beantworten Sie die Fragen zum Text.
Welche Lösung ist die richtige?

1. Why does Rebus think that people talk at the casino?
   a) Because it's a relaxing place to be.
   b) Because they know they won't be overheard.
   c) Because the croupiers will listen to them.

2. What is Matty's reaction when he sees the red light?
   a) He skids to a halt.
   b) He thinks about braking but then accelerates.
   c) He sounds his horn.

Just missed the cyclist. The guy was coming through on green and had to twist his front wheel hard to avoid contact, then teetered and fell on to the road. Matty's foot eased off the accelerator, thought about the brake, then went back on the accelerator again.

bei Grün • drehen • schwankte • Matty fuhr langsamer • Streifenwagen

That's when he saw the cop car. And thought: I can't afford this.

They'd breathalysed him and taken him to St Leonard's, where he'd sat around and let the machinery chew him up. Would it come to a trial? Would there be a report in the papers? How could he keep his name from getting around? He'd worked himself up into a right state by the time Detective Inspector John Rebus had sat down across from him.

ins Röhrchen pusten lassen • Würde es vor Gericht kommen? • sich furchtbar aufgeregt

'I can't afford this,' Matty had blurted out.

herausgeplatzt

'Sorry?'

He'd swallowed and tried to find a story. 'I work in a casino. Any black mark against me, they'll boot me out. Look, if it's a question of compensation or anything … like, I'll buy him a new bike.'

Minuspunkt • mich rausschmeißen • Entschädigung • Trunkenheit am Steuer • eine rote Ampel überfahren

Rebus had picked up a sheet of paper. 'Drunk driving … in a borrowed car you weren't insured to drive … running a red light … leaving the scene of an accident

3. What is Matty's reaction after he just misses the cyclist?
   a) He stops the car and gets out.
   b) He slows down and turns the car around.
   c) He slows down and then speeds up again.

4. What does Matty offer to do to avoid going to trial?
   a) He offers Rebus a bribe of five hundred pounds.
   b) He offers to buy the cyclist a new bike.
   c) He promises never to drink and drive again.

hatte den Kopf geschüttelt	…' Rebus had shaken his head, read the sheet through one more time and then put it down, and looked up at Matty. 'What casino did you say you work for?'
Visitenkarten	Later, he'd given Matty two business cards, both with his phone number.

angewidert •	'The first one's for you to tear up in disgust,' he'd said.
Abgemacht?	'The other one's to keep. Have we got a deal?'
	'Look, Mr Rebus,' Matty said now, as the car stopped for lights on Raeburn Place, 'I'm doing the best I can.'
hinter den Kulissen	'I want to know what's happening behind the scenes at the Morvena.'
	'I wouldn't know.'
	'Anything at all, it doesn't matter how small it seems. Any stories, gossip, anything overheard. Ever seen the owner entertain people in his office? Maybe open the place for a private party? Names, faces, anything at all. Put your mind to it, Matty. Just put your mind to it.'
Hast du je mitbekommen, dass der Besitzer …	
Gäste hat? •	'They'd skin me alive.'
denk mal scharf darüber nach •	'Who's they?'
	Matty swallowed. 'Mr Mandelson.'
mir den Kopf abreißen	'He's the owner, right?'
	'Right.'

Übung 37   Setzen Sie das Verb in den folgenden Sätzen jeweils in die Zeit-form, die in Klammern steht.

1. Rebus reads the sheet through one more time. (Imperfekt)

2. He gives Matty two business cards. (Plusquamperfekt)

3. Rebus goes over the Forth Bridge to Fife. (Imperfekt)

4. The police have found Damon. (Futur)

5. Janis is Rebus's girlfriend. (Imperfekt)

6. Rebus drops Matty at the foot of Broughton Street. (Perfekt)

7. None of the staff at the club has seen the woman in the photo. (Imperfekt)

'On paper at least. What I need to know is who might be pulling his strings.'

'I can't see anyone pulling his strings.'

'You'd be surprised. Hard bastard, is he?'

'I'd say so.'

'Given you grief?' Matty shook his head. 'Do you see much of him?' 'Not much,' Matty said. Not, he might have added, until recently at any rate. Rebus dropped him at the foot of Broughton Street, headed back up to Leith Walk and along York Place on to Queen Street. He passed the casino again and slowed, a frown on his face. At the next set of lights, he did a U-turn so he could be sure. Yes, it was the Roller from Gaitanos, no doubt about it. Parked outside the Morvena.

auf dem Papier

• seine Fäden in der Hand haben könnte •

knallhart •

Hat er dir Kummer gemacht? •

setzte ... ab •

fuhr ... zurück

stirnrunzelnd •

wendete

Six

'Mind if I join you?'

Rebus was eating breakfast in the canteen and wishing there was more caffeine in the coffee, or more coffee in the coffee come to that. He nodded to the empty chair and Siobhan sat down.

'Heavy night?' she said.

'Believe it or not, I was on orange juice.'

Darf ich mich zu dir setzen?

Zu viel getrunken gestern Abend?

• habe ...

getrunken

8. Rebus drank orange juice all evening. (Präsens)

9. Rebus takes Matty for a drive around the town. (Imperfekt)

10. Siobhan sits down at Rebus's table. (Imperfekt)

11. Matty does the best he can. (Perfekt)

12. Matty shook his head. (Präsens)

13. Rebus tells Siobhan about the case. (Futur)

14. Mr Mackenzie does not like Rebus. (Imperfekt)

at all events – auf alle Fälle

und spülte ihn ... hinunter	She bit into her muffin, washing it down with milk. 'Harry tells me you had him working a tape.'
	'Harry?'
Das ist mir neu.	'Our video wizard. He said it was a missing person. News to me.'
	'It's not official. The son of an old schoolfriend of mine.'
	'Standing at a bar one minute and gone the next?'
Harry ist eine große Klatschbase.	Rebus looked at her and she smiled. 'Harry's a great one for gossip.'
	'I'm working on it in my own time.'
	'Need any help?'
Kannst du zufällig gut mit einer Kristallkugel umgehen?	'Handy with a crystal ball, are you?' But Rebus dug into his pocket and brought out the still from the video. 'That's Damon there,' he said, pointing.
	'Who's that with him?'
	'I wish I knew. She's not with him. I don't know who she is.'
	'You've asked around?'
	'I was at the club last night. A few punters remembered her.'
Geschlecht	'Male punters?' She waited till Rebus nodded. 'You were asking the wrong sex. Any man would have given

---

Vervollständigen Sie die folgenden Sätze mit den Wörtern in Klammern.

(wizard, sex, muffin, schoolfriend, at the club, pocket, great one)

1. Siobhan washes her _____ down with milk.

2. Harry is the video _____.

3. Damon is the son of an old _____ of Rebus's.

4. Harry is a _____ for gossip.

5. Rebus brings out the photo from his _____.

6. Rebus was _____ last night.

7. Siobhan thinks Rebus was asking the wrong _____.

her the once-over, but only superficially. A woman, on the other hand, would have seen her as competition. Have you never noticed women in nightclubs? They've got eyes like lasers. Plus, what if she visited the loo*?' Rebus was interested now. 'What if she did?'

'*That's* where women talk. Maybe someone spoke to her, maybe she said something back. Ears would have been listening.' Siobhan stared at the photo. 'Funny, it's almost like she's got an aura.'

'How do you mean?'

'Like she's shining.'

'Interior light.'

'Exactly.'

'No, that's what your friend Harry said. It's the interior lighting that gives that effect.'

'Maybe he didn't know what he was saying.'

'I'm not sure I know what *you're* saying.'

'Some religions believe in spirit guides. They're supposed to lead you to the next world.'

'You mean this one's not the end?'

She smiled. 'Depends on your religion.'

'Well, it's plenty enough for me.' He looked at the photo again.

hätte sie mit einem Blick abgeschätzt • Konkurrenz • aufs Klo gegangen ist
Inneres Licht.
Innenbeleuchtung
Geisterführer
mehr als genug

Es gibt in Großbritannien sehr viele Wörter für „Toilette". Natürlich wählt man den zur Situation passenden Begriff. Loo zum Beispiel ist weit verbreitet und ziemlich neutral, aber umgangssprachlich. Wenn man sehr höflich sein will, sagt man toilet, WC oder lavatory, und wenn man alles andere als höflich sein will, benutzt man bog. Es gibt auch eine große Auswahl euphemistischer Wendungen, die man verwenden kann, wenn man mal muss. Zum Beispiel: I have to spend a penny, I have to pay a visit, und für Frauen I have to powder my nose.

ich habe eigentlich nur Spaß gemacht

'I was sort of joking, you know, about her being a spirit guide.'

'I know.'

(= Old House)

hineingestellt

He met with Helen Cousins that night. They spoke over a drink in the Auld Hoose. Rebus hadn't been in the place in quarter of a century, and there'd been changes. They'd installed a pool table.

Verlobungsring

• Knöchel •

leblos

'You weren't invited along that night?' Rebus asked her. She shook her head. She was twenty, three years younger than Damon. The fingers of her right hand played with her engagement ring, rolling it, sliding it off over the knuckle and then back down again. She had short, lifeless brown hair, dark, tired eyes, and acne around her mouth. 'I was out with the girls. See, that was how we played it. One night a week the boys would go off on their own, and we'd go somewhere else. Then another night we'd all get together.'

zusammen-kommen

hüpfte ... auf •

bückte sich

'Do you know anyone who was at Gaitanos that night? Apart from Damon and his pals?' She chewed her bottom lip while considering. The ring came off her finger and bounced once before hitting the floor. She stooped to pick it up.

Der Satz aus dem Text „You weren't invited along that night?" steht im Passiv. Das Passiv wird mit der entsprechenden Zeitform des Verbs to be und dem Partizip Perfekt gebildet. Setzen Sie die Verben in den folgenden Sätzen wie im Beispiel ins Passiv.

Beispiel: His mother telephoned him.
          He was telephoned by his mother.

1. Rebus bought the girls a round of drinks.
2. The owners of the pub had installed a pool table.
3. The police have not found Damon.
4. Rebus has been questioning Mr Mackenzie.

'It's always doing that.'

'You better watch it, you're going to lose it.'

She pushed the ring back on. 'Yes,' she said, 'Corinne and Jacky were there.'

'Corinne and Jacky?' She nodded. 'Where can I find them?'

A phone call brought them to the Auld Hoose. Rebus got in the round: Bacardi and Coke for Corinne, Bacardi and blackcurrant for Jacky, a second vodka and orange for Helen and another bottle of no-alcohol lager for himself. He eyed the optics behind the bar. His mean little drink was costing more than a whisky. Something was telling him to indulge in a Teacher's. Maybe it's my spirit guide, he thought, dismissing the idea.

Corinne had long black hair crimped with curling tongs. Her pal Jacky was tiny, with dyed platinum hair. When he got back to the table, they were in a huddle, exchanging gossip. Rebus took out the photograph again.

'Look,' Corinne said, 'there's Damon.' So they all had a good look. Then Rebus touched his finger to the strapless aura.

kaufte

alkoholfreies helles Bier • schaute auf • Portionierer • kärglich • sich ... zu gönnen • (Whiskymarke) • das sie mit dem Lockenstab gewellt hatte • platinblond • saßen sie eng zusammengedrängt • schulterfrei

5. Two men at the club saw the blond woman that night.

6. Rebus drives Matty around the town.

7. Matty has written down the name of the suspect.

8. Mrs Playfair asked Rebus about his family.

9. The bouncer is protecting Mr Mackenzie.

10. Siobhan has joined Rebus at his table.

11. Rebus tells Damon's parents about the case.

12. Rebus had seen the Rolls-Royce before.

'Remember her?'

Helen prickled visibly. 'Who is she?'

zuckte sichtlich zusammen

'Yeah, she was there,' Jacky said.

'Was she with anyone?'

'Didn't see her up dancing.'

'Isn't that why people go to clubs?'

'Well, it's one reason.' All three broke into a giggle.

fingen an zu kichern

'You didn't speak to her?'

'No.'

'Not even in the toilets?'

hat sich die Augen geschminkt

'I saw her in there,' Corinne said. 'She was doing her eyes.'

'Did she say anything?'

hochnäsig •
versnobt

'She seemed sort of … stuck-up.' 'Snobby,' Jacky agreed. Rebus tried to think of another question and couldn't. They ignored him for a while as they exchanged news. It was like they hadn't seen each other in a year. At one point, Helen got up to use the toilet. Rebus expected the other two to accompany her, but only Corinne did so. He sat with Jacky for a moment, then, for want of anything else to say, asked her what she thought of Damon. He meant about Damon disappearing, but she didn't take it that way.

weil ihm nichts anderes einfiel •
sie verstand es nicht so

Übung 40

Sind die folgenden Aussagen wahr oder falsch?
Tragen Sie ein T für true oder ein F für false in die Kästchen ein.

1. The girls don't remember seeing the woman in the photo at the club.
2. Corinne saw the woman doing her make-up in the toilets.
3. The girls think that the woman in the photo looked friendly.
4. Corinne stays with Rebus while the other two women go to the toilet.
5. Rebus asks Jacky what she thinks of the club.

'Ach, he's all right.'

'Just all right?'

'Well, you know, Damon's heart's in the right place, but he's a bit thick. A bit slow, I mean.'

'Really?' The impression Rebus had received from Damon's family had been of a genius-in-waiting. He suddenly realised just how superficial his own portrait of Damon was. Siobhan's words should have been warning – so far he'd heard only one side of Damon. 'Helen likes him though?'

'I suppose so.'

'They're engaged.'

'It happens, doesn't it? I've got friends who got engaged just so they could throw a party.' She looked around the bar, then leaned towards him. 'They used to have some mega arguments.'

'What about?'

'Jealousy, I suppose. She'd see him notice someone, or he'd say she'd been letting some guy chat her up. Just the usual.' She turned the photo around so it faced her. 'She looks like a dream, doesn't she? I remember she was dressed to kill. Made the rest of us spit.'

'But you'd never seen her before?'

Damon hat das
Herz auf dem
rechten Fleck •
doof •
künftiges Genie
• oberflächlich •
Bild

Ich denke
schon. • verlobt
• sich verloben
• eine Party
schmeißen

Eifersucht •
sie anmacht •
traumhaft •
aufgedonnert •
es hat ... uns
angekotzt

6. Jacky thinks Damon is a bit stupid.

7. Damon's family had given Rebus the impression that Damon was a bit stupid too.

8. Rebus realises that he doesn't know much about Damon.

9. Helen and Damon are getting engaged.

10. Helen and Damon were always arguing about money.

11. The woman in the photo is dressed very attractively.

12. The other women are very jealous of her.

Jacky shook her head. No, no one seemed to have seen her before, nobody knew who she was. Unlikely then that she was local.

unwahr-scheinlich

'Were there any buses in that night?'

'That doesn't happen at Gaitanos,' she told him. 'It's not "in" enough any more. There's a new place in Dunfermline. That gets the busloads.' Jacky tapped the photo. 'You think she's gone off with Damon?'

Busladungen
Kunden • klopfte
auf

Rebus looked at her and saw behind the eyeliner to a sharp intelligence. 'It's possible,' he said quietly.

'I don't think so,' she said. 'She wouldn't be interested, and he wouldn't have had the guts.'

ihm hätte der
Schneid gefehlt

On his way home, Rebus dropped into St Leonard's. The amount he was paying in bridge tolls, he was thinking about a season ticket. There was a fax on his desk. He'd been promised it in the afternoon, but there'd been a delay. It identified the owner of the Rolls-Royce as a Mr Richard Mandelson, with an address in Juniper Green. Mr Mandelson had no criminal record outstanding, whether for motoring offences or anything else. Rebus tried to imagine some poor parking warden trying to give the Roller a ticket with

• schaute kurz
bei ... vorbei •
Dauerkarte

es hatte sich
verspätet •
war nicht vorbe-
straft • Vekehrs-
delikte •
Politesse

Übung 41 Die folgenden Sätze enthalten jeweils einen grammatischen Fehler. Suchen und korrigieren Sie ihn.

1. Nobody knew who the woman were.
2. Jacky asks Rebus if he thinks the woman has gone up with Damon.
3. Jacky doesn't think the woman would have been interesting in Damon.
4. Rebus had been promised the fax on the afternoon.
5. Mr Mandelson don't have a criminal record.
6. Mr Mandelson used be a casino manager.

the fat man behind the wheel. There were a few more facts about Mr Mandelson, including last known occupation. Casino manager.

am Steuer • Beschäftigung

Seven

Matty and Stevie Scoular saw one another socially now. Stevie would sometimes phone and invite Matty to some party or dinner, or just for a drink. At the same time as Matty was flattered, he did wonder what Stevie's angle was, had even come out and asked him.

trafen sich privat

geschmeichelt • was … im Schilde führte • ihn … offen gefragt • Depp

'I mean,' he'd said, 'I'm just a toe-rag from the school playground, and you … well, you're Super Stevie, you're the king.'

'Aye, if you believe the papers.' Stevie had finished his drink – Perrier, he had a game the next day. 'I don't know, Matty, maybe it's that I miss all that.'

'All what?'

'Schooldays. It was a laugh back then, wasn't it?'

es hat Spaß gemacht • würden alles dafür geben

Matty had frowned, not really remembering. 'But the life you've got now, Stevie, man. People would kill for it.'

And Stevie had nodded, looking suddenly sad.

Another time, a couple of kids had asked Stevie for his

7. The fax gives Rebus a few more facts from Mr Mandelson.

8. Matty and Stevie was seeing each other socially.

9. Stevie would sometimes invite Matty to a drink.

10. Stevie is considered to be the kings of football.

11. Matty has saw Stevie in the newspapers.

12. Stevie misses her schooldays.

13. Matty can't really remembering his time at school.

14. Matty enjoy going out with Stevie.

Autogramm

eine Lektion in
Demut • ver-
stand ... es nicht
• Druck •
alles

hübsch

saugte es alles
auf

ihn ... fallen las-
sen • Ablenkung
• die Geschichten
im Gedächtnis
abzulegen • und
verschönerte •
BMW

autograph, then had turned and asked Matty for his, thinking that whoever he was, he had to be somebody. Stevie had laughed at that, said something about it being a lesson in humility. Again, Matty didn't get it. There were times when Stevie seemed to be on a different planet. Maybe it was understandable, the pressure he was under. Stevie seemed to remember a lot more about school than Matty did: teachers' names, the lot. They talked about Gullane, too, what a boring place to grow up. Sometimes they didn't talk much at all. Just took out a couple of dolls: Stevie would always bring one along for Matty. She wouldn't be quite as gorgeous as Stevie's, but that was all right. Matty could understand that. He was soaking it all up, enjoying it while it lasted. He had half an idea that Stevie and him would be best friends for life, and another that Stevie would dump him soon and find some other distraction. He thought Stevie needed him right now much more than *he* needed Stevie. So he soaked up what he could, started filing the stories away for future use, tweaking them here and there ...

Tonight they took in a couple of bars, a bit of a drive in Stevie's Beamer: he preferred BMWs to Porsches, more

---

Übung 42   Beantworten Sie die Fragen zum Text.

1. What did the kids ask Stevie and Matty for?

2. What, for example, does Stevie remember about school?

3. What do the two men think of Gullane?

4. What was different about the girls Stevie brought along for Matty compared to his own?

5. Why does Stevie prefer BMWs to Porsches?

6. Why don't the two men stay at the club for very long?

7. Where does Stevie drop Matty off?

space for passengers. They ended up at a club, but did-n't stay long. Stevie had a game the next day. He was always very conscientious that way: Perrier and early nights. Stevie dropped Matty off outside his flat, sounding the horn as he roared away. Matty hadn't spotted the other car, but he heard a door opening, looked across the road and recognised Malibu straight off. Malibu was Mr Mandelson's driver. He'd eased him-self out of the Roller and was holding open the back door while looking over to Matty.

landeten
schließlich in •
gewissenhaft •
früh ins Bett •
losbrauste

sofort •
hatte sich aus …
herausgehievt

So Matty crossed the street. As he did so, he walked into Malibu's shadow, cast by the sodium street lamp. At that moment, though he didn't know what was about to happen, he realised he was lost.

den die … warf
• Natrium-

'Get in, Matty.'

The voice, of course, was Mandelson's. Matty got into the car and Malibu closed the door after him, then kept guard outside. They weren't going anywhere.

stand … Wache

'Ever been in a Roller before, Matty?'

'I don't think so.'

'You'd remember if you had. I could have had one years back, but only by buying secondhand. I wanted to wait until I had the cash for a nice new one. That leather

vor Jahren •
aus zweiter
Hand • Kohle

8. How does Matty realise that Mr Mandelson's car is parked over the road?

9. What does Malibu do for a living?

10. What does Malibu do after Matty has got into the car?

11. What sort of Rolls-Royce could Mr Mandelson have bought before now?

12. What sort of Rolls-Royce can he afford to buy now?

smell – you don't get it with any other car.' Mandelson lit a cigar. The windows were closed and the car started filling with sour smoke. 'Know how I came to afford a
nagelneu — brand new Roller, Matty?'

'Hard work?' Matty's mouth was dry. Cars, he thought: Rebus's, Stevie's, and now this one. Plus, of course, the one he'd borrowed that night, the one that had brought him to this.

'Don't be stupid. My dad worked thirty years in a shop, six days a week and he still couldn't have made the
Anzahlung • — down-payment. Faith, Matty, that's the key. You have
Vertrauen • to believe in yourself, and sometimes you have to trust
vertrauen other people – strangers some of them, or people you
• das Spiel, das don't like, people it's hard to trust. That's the gamble
das Leben mit life's making with you, and if you place your bet,
einem spielt • sometimes you get lucky. Except it's not luck – not
setzt • Gewinn- entirely. See, there are odds, like in every game, and
chancen • that's where judgment comes in. I like to think I'm a
Urteilsvermögen good judge of character.'

Only now did Mandelson turn to look at him. There seemed to Matty to be nothing behind the eyes, noth-
weil ihm nichts ing at all.
Besseres einfiel 'Yes, sir,' he said, for want of anything better.

Übung 43 — Einige Substantive im Englischen haben unregelmäßige Pluralformen. Ein Beispiel im Text ist people, die Pluralform von person. Bilden Sie die Pluralformen der folgenden Wörter. Einige sind regelmäßig und einige unregelmäßig.

child	table
story	tooth
video	sheep
bus	lorry
mouse	life
man	foot

'That was Stevie dropped you off, eh?' Matty nodded. 'Now, your man Stevie, he's got something else, something we haven't discussed yet. He's got a gift. He's had to work, of course, but the thing was there to begin with. Don't ask me where it came from or why it should have been given to him in particular – that's one for the philosophers, and I don't claim to be a philosopher. What I am is a businessman … and a gambler. Only I don't bet on nags* or dogs* or a turn of the cards, I bet on people. I'm betting on you, Matty.'
'Me?'

Mandelson nodded, barely visible inside the cloud of smoke. 'I want you to talk to Stevie on my behalf. I want you to get him to do me a favour.'

Matty rubbed his forehead with his fingers. He knew what was coming but didn't want to hear it.

'I saw a recent interview,' Mandelson went on, 'where he told the reporter he always gave a hundred and ten per cent. All I want is to knock maybe twenty per cent off for next Saturday's game. You know what I'm saying?'

Next Saturday … An away tie at Kirkcaldy. Stevie expected to run rings around the Raith Rovers defence.

Gabe

ausgerechnet
ihm • behaupte

Pferde • das
Umdrehen der
Karten

für mich •
mir einen Gefal-
len zu tun • rieb

20% weniger zu
geben •
Auswärtsspiel •
• in die Tasche
zu stecken

Der Pferderennsport ist auch in Großbritannien und Irland sehr populär. Anders als in Deutschland gibt es hauptsächlich Jagdrennen (über Hindernisse) und Galopprennen. Trabrennen findet man eher in den USA. Die Einsätze der Kunden bei den Buchmachern tragen den Hauptteil der Kosten in diesem Sport. Genauso wie auf Pferde kann man in Großbritannien auch auf Windhunde wetten. Bei dieser Art Rennsport jagen Windhunde einen künstlichen Hasen um eine Rennbahn.

info

'He won't do it,' Matty said. 'Come to that, neither will I.'

'No?' Mandelson laughed. A hand landed on Matty's thigh. 'You fucked up in London, son. They knew you'd end up taking a croupier's job somewhere else, it's the only thing you know how to do. So they phoned around, and eventually they phoned *me*. I told them I'd never heard of you. That can change, Matty. Want me to talk to them again?'

'I'd tell them you lied to them the first time.'

Mandelson shrugged. 'I can live with that. But what do you think they'll do to *you*, Matty? They were pretty angry about whatever scheme it was you pulled. I'd say they were furious.'

Matty felt like he was going to heave. He was sweating, his lungs toxic. 'He won't do it,' he said again.

'Be persuasive, Matty. You're his friend. Remind him that his tab's up to three and a half. All he has to do is ease off for one game, and the tab's history. And Matty, I'll know if you've talked to him or not, so no games, eh? Or you might find yourself with no place left to hide.'

Margin glossary:
hast ... Scheiß gemacht • dass du letztlich ... annehmen würdest

zuckte mit den Schultern • Ding, das du gedreht hast • wütend • kotzen • voller Gift • überrede ihn • Rechnung • nachzulassen • die Rechnung ist Geschichte

Übung 44   Die folgende Zusammenfassung des Textes auf dieser Seite enthält drei sachliche Fehler. Können Sie sie finden und korrigieren?

Matty tells Mr Mandelson that neither he nor Stevie will do as he asks. However, Mr Mandelson has a way to blackmail Matty. He has been contacted by Matty's former employers in Manchester who want to find Matty. Mr Mandelson told them he didn't know him but now threatens to tell them where Matty is. Matty threatens to tell them that Mr Mandelson lied and this makes Mr Mandelson feel frightened. He urges Matty to persuade Stevie not to play well for three games.

Eight

Rebus searched his flat, but came up with only half a   entdeckte •
dozen snapshots: two of his ex-wife Rhona, posing   die ... posierte
with Samantha, their daughter, back when Sammy was
seven or eight; two further shots of Sammy in her   im Teenageralter
teens; one showing his father as a young man, kissing
the woman who would become Rebus's mother; and a
final photograph, a family grouping, showing uncles,
aunts and cousins whose names Rebus didn't know.
There were other photographs, of course – at least,
there had been – but not here, not in the flat. He
guessed Rhona still kept some, maybe his brother   nahm an
Michael had the others. But they could be anywhere.
Rebus hadn't thought of himself as the kind to spend   hatte sich nicht
long nights with the family album, using it as a crutch   für einen gehal-
to memory, always with the fear that remembrance   ten, der • Stütze
would yield to sentiment.   • der Sentimen-
If I died tonight, he thought, what would I bequeath to   talität weichen
the world? Looking around, the answer was: nothing.   würde • hinter-
The thought scared him, and worst of all it made him   lassen
want a drink, and not just one drink but a dozen.
Instead of which, he drove north back into Fife. It had
been overcast all day, and the evening was warm. He   bewölkt

Auf welches Wort oder welchen Satz im Text beziehen sich die   **Übung 45**
folgenden Erklärungen?

1. a book in which you keep stamps etc
2. the child of your aunt or uncle
3. a group of twelve of the same thing
4. a set of rooms for living in on one floor of a building
5. to make someone feel frightened
6. a photograph taken quickly

herzlich wenig	didn't know what he was doing, knew he had precious little to say to either of Damon's parents, and yet that's
im Sinn	where he ended up. He'd had the destination in mind all along.
machte auf •	Brian Mee answered the door, wearing a smart suit
zu binden •	and just finishing knotting his tie.
Geht ihr aus?	'Sorry, Brian,' Rebus said. 'Are you off out?'
	'In ten minutes. Come in anyway. Is it Damon?'
Spannung •	Rebus shook his head and saw the tension in Brian's
Erleichterung •	face turn to relief. Yes, a visit in person wouldn't be
persönlich	good news, would it? Good news had to be given immediately by telephone, not by a knock at the door.
Überbringer	Rebus should have realised; he'd been the bearer of bad news often enough in his time.
	'Sorry, Brian,' he repeated. They were in the hallway. Janis's voice came from above, asking who it was.
	'It's Johnny,' her husband called back. Then to Rebus, 'It's all right to call you that?'
schlecht behan-	'Of course. It's my name, isn't it?' He could have added:
delt • nicht	again, after all this time. He looked at Brian, remem-
dass es Barney	bering the way they'd sometimes mistreated him at
etwas auszu-	school: not that 'Barney' had seemed to mind, but
machen schien	who could tell for sure? And then that night of the last

Übung 46   Setzen Sie die Verben in den folgenden Sätzen in die passende Verlaufsform wie im Beispiel.

Beispiel: Rebus speaks to Brian.
              Rebus is speaking to Brian.

1. Rebus goes to see Brian and Janis.
2. Brian wore a smart suit and tie.
3. Brian and Janis will leave soon.
4. They have waited for news from Rebus.

school dance … Brian had been there for Mitch. Brian had been there; Rebus had not. He'd been too busy losing Janis, and losing consciousness.

She was coming downstairs now. 'I'll be back in a sec,' Brian said, heading up past her.

'You look terrific,' Rebus told her. The blue dress was well-chosen, her make-up highlighting all the right features of her busy face. She managed a smile.

'No news?'

'Sorry,' he said again. 'Just thought I'd see how you are.'

'Oh, we're pining away.' Another smile, tinged by shame this time. 'It's a dinner-dance, we bought the tickets months back. It's for the Jolly Beggars*.'

'Nobody expects you to sit at home every night, Janis.'

'But all the same …' Her cheeks grew flushed and her eyes sought his. 'We're not going to find him, are we?'

'Not easily. Our best bet's that he'll get in touch.'

'If he can,' she said quietly.

'Come on, Janis.' He put his hands on her shoulders, like they were strangers and about to dance. 'You might hear from him tomorrow, or it might take months.'

Bewusstsein • Moment • als er die Treppe … hinaufging • hob … hervor • Züge • unruhig

wir vergehen vor Gram • mit einem Anflug von • Abend-gesellschaft mit Tanz • erröteten • Er wird sich höchstens selbst melden.

5. Janis had got ready upstairs.

6. Janis came downstairs.

7. Janis wears a blue dress.

8. Rebus will drive home soon.

The Jolly Beggars, der Titel einer Cantata des schottischen Nationaldichters Robert Burns, gab einer zeitgenössischen Band den Namen.

info

inzwischen •

'And meantime life goes on, eh?'

So ungefähr. •

'Something like that.'

blinzelte ihre
Tränen weg

She smiled again, blinking back tears. 'Why don't you come with us, John?'

Rebus dropped his hands from her shoulders. 'I haven't danced in years.'

aus der Übung

'So you'd be rusty.'

'Thanks, Janis, but not tonight.'

'Know something? I bet they play the same records we used to dance to at school.'

It was his turn to smile. Brian was coming back downstairs, patting his hair into place.

'You'd be welcome to join us, Johnny,' he said.

Verabredung

'I've another appointment, Brian. Maybe next time, eh?'

'Let's make that a promise.'

gab ihm einen
flüchtigen Kuss
auf die Wange

They went out to their cars together. Janis pecked him on the cheek, Brian shook his hand. He watched them drive off then headed to the cemetery.

It was dark, and the gates were locked, so Rebus sat in his car and smoked a cigarette. He thought about his parents and the rest of his family and remembered sto-

untrennbar

ries about Bowhill, stories which seemed inextricable

Übung 47   Beantworten Sie die Fragen zum Text.
Welche Lösung ist die richtige?

1. What excuse does Rebus give Brian for not going dancing?
   a) He is too drunk to dance.
   b) He isn't wearing the right clothes.
   c) He has another appointment.

2. What does Janis do to Rebus before she drives away?
   a) She kisses him.
   b) She gives him a hug.
   c) She shakes his hand.

from family history: mining tragedies; a girl found drowned in the River Ore; a holiday car crash which had erased an entire family. Then there was Johnny Thomson, Celtic goalkeeper, injured during an 'Old Firm' match. He was in his early twenties when he died, and was buried behind those gates, not far from Rebus's parents. *Not Dead, But at Rest in the Arms of the Lord*. The Lord had to be a bodybuilder.

From family he turned to friends and tried recalling a dozen names to put to faces he remembered from schooldays. Other friends: people he'd known in the army, the SAS. All the people he'd dealt with during his career in the police. Villains he'd put away, some who'd slipped through his fingers. People he'd interviewed, suspected, questioned, broken the worst kind of news to. Acquaintances from the Oxford Bar and all the other pubs where he'd ever been a regular. Local shopkeepers. Jesus, the list was endless. All these people who'd played a part in his life, in shaping who he was and how he acted, how he felt about things. All of them, out there somewhere and nowhere, gathered together only inside his head. And chief among them tonight, Brian and Janis.

Grubenunglücke • Autounfall • ausgelöscht • Torwart • verletzt • Spiels zwischen Celtic und Rangers • begraben • wandte er sich ... zu • die er in Verbindung mit Gesichtern bringen konnte • Spezialeinheit der Armee • Verbrecher • eingesperrt • mitgeteilt • Bekannte • Stammgast • Ladenbesitzer

an vorderster Front

3. Who was Johnny Thomson?
   a) Rebus's cousin.
   b) A villain Rebus put in prison.
   c) A footballer.

4. What is the name of the pub at which Rebus is a regular?
   a) The Red Lion.
   b) The Oxford Bar.
   c) The Black Bull.

That night of the school dance … It was true he'd been drunk – elated. He'd felt he could *do* anything, *be* anything. Because he'd come to a decision that day – he wouldn't join the army, he'd stay in Bowhill with Janis, apply for a job at the dockyard. His dad had told him not to be so stupid – 'short-sighted' was the word he'd used. But what did parents know about their children's desires? So he'd drunk some beer and headed off to the dance, his thoughts only of Janis. Tonight he'd tell her. And Mitch, of course. He'd have to tell Mitch, tell him he'd be heading into the army alone. But Mitch wouldn't mind, he'd understand, as best friends had to.

But while Rebus had been outside with Janis, his friend Mitch was being cornered by four teenagers who considered themselves his enemies. This was their last chance for revenge, and they'd gone in hard, kicking and punching. Four against one … until Barney had waded in, shrugging off blows, and dragged Mitch to safety. But one kick had done the damage, dislodging a retina. Mitch's vision stayed fuzzy in that eye for a few days, then disappeared. And where had Rebus been? Out cold on the concrete by the bike sheds.

And why had he never thanked Barney Mee?

Marginal glossary:
in Hochstimmung • zu einem Entschluss gekommen • sich um … bewerben • kurzsichtig • Wünsche

wurde … in die Enge getrieben • sie hatten hart angegriffen • sich eingemischt hatte • ignoriert hatte • und hatte die Netzhaut gelöst • verschwommen • bewusstlos

---

Übung 48   Ordnen Sie den folgenden Wörtern aus dem Text die passende deutsche Übersetzung zu.

drunk	Schlag
enemy	Sehvermögen
revenge	Feind
blow	Tritt
kick	Beton
vision	betrunken
concrete	Rache

He blinked now and sniffed, wondering if he was coming down with a cold. He'd had this idea when he came back to Bowhill that the place would seem beyond redemption, that he'd be able to tell himself it had lost its sense of community, become just another town for him to pass through. Maybe he'd wanted to put it behind him. Well, it hadn't worked. He got out of the car and looked around. The street was dead. He reached up and hauled himself over the iron railings and walked a circuit of the cemetery for an hour or so, and felt strangely at peace.

schniefte • sich erkältet hatte • hoffnungslos verloren • Gemeinschafts- sinn • es hinter sich bringen • es hatte nicht geklappt • zog • Zaun • ging eine Runde • ruhig

Nine

'So what's the panic, Matty?'
After a home draw with Rangers, Stevie was ready for a night on the town. One-one, and of course he'd scored his team's only goal. The reporters would be busy filing their copy, saying for the umpteenth time that he was his side's hero, that without him they were a very ordinary team indeed. Rangers had known that: Stevie's marker had been out for blood, sliding studs-first into tackles which Stevie had done his damnedest to avoid. He'd come out of the game with a couple of fresh

Heimunentschie- den gegen • 1:1 • ihre Berichte zu schreiben • x-ten • Manndecker • mit den Stollen voraus • sich alle Mühe gegeben hatte

blink	Mannschaft
iron	schießen
cemetery	blinzeln
goal	Angriff
score	Held
hero	Tor
team	Eisen
tackle	Friedhof

bruises and grazes, a nick on one knee but, to his manager's all too palpable relief, fit to play again midweek.

'I said what's the panic?'

blaue Flecken •
Abschürfungen
• kleine Schnitt-
wunde • spürbar

Matty had worried himself sleepless. He knew he had several options. Speak to Stevie, that was one of them. Another was not to speak to him, but tell Mandelson he had. Then it would be down to whether or not Mandelson believed him. Option three: do a runner; only Mandelson was right about that – he was running out of places to hide. With *two* casino bosses out for his blood, how could he ever pick up another croupier's job?

• bis er nicht
mehr schlafen
konnte • käme
es darauf an,
ob • abhauen
• die es auf ihn
abgesehen hatten

If he spoke with Stevie, he'd lose a new-found friend. But to stay silent … well, there was very little percentage in it. So here he was in Stevie's flat, having demanded to see him. In the corner, a TV was replaying a tape of the afternoon's match. There was no commentary, just the sounds of the terraces and the dugouts.

das würde
nichts bringen

Kommentar •
Trainerbänke

'No panic,' he said now, playing for time.

Stevie stared at him. 'You all right? Want a drink or something?'

'Maybe a vodka.'

Übung 49   Finden Sie die Wörter oder Sätze im Text, die das gleiche bedeuten wie die folgenden Begriffe:

1. possibility
2. fear
3. occupation
4. quiet
5. noise
6. to ask

'Anything in it?'

'I'll take it as it comes.' pur

Stevie poured him a drink. Matty had been here half an hour now, and they still hadn't talked. The telephone had hardly stopped: reporters' questions, family and friends offering congratulations. Stevie had shrugged off the superlatives.

Matty took the drink, swallowed it, wondering if he schluckte ihn
could still walk away. Then he remembered Malibu, hinunter
and saw shadows falling.

'Thing is, Stevie,' he said. 'You know my boss at the die Sache ist die
Morvena, Mr Mandelson?'

'I owe him money, of course I know him.' schulde

'He says we could do something about that.'

'What? My tab?' Stevie was checking himself in the
mirror, having changed into his on-the-town clothes. feine Klamotten
'I don't get it,' he said.

Well, Stevie, Matty thought, it was nice knowing you,
pal. 'All you have to do is ease off next Saturday.' Beim Auswärts-

Stevie frowned and turned from the mirror. 'Away to spiel gegen
Raith?' He came and sat down opposite Matty. 'He told Raith? •
you to tell me?' He waited till Matty nodded. 'That bas- Was hat er
tard. What's in it for him?' davon?

Ersetzen Sie alle Substantive und Namen in den folgenden Sätzen **Übung 50**
durch die entsprechenden Personalpronomen.

Beispiel: Stevie poured Matty a drink.

He poured it for him.

1. The reporters ask Stevie about the match.
2. Matty is frightened of Mr Mandelson and Malibu.
3. Janis and Brian invite Rebus to go out dancing.
4. Siobhan helps Rebus with his cases.
5. Damon hasn't written to Janis and Brian.
6. Matty gives the message to Stevie.

Matty wriggled on the leather sofa. 'I've been thinking about it. Raith are going through a bad patch, but you know yourself that if you're taken out of the equation …'

'Then they'd be up against not very much. My boss has told everybody to get the ball to me. If they spend the whole game doing that and I don't do anything with it …'

Matty nodded. 'What I think is, the odds will be on you scoring. Nobody'll be expecting Raith to put one in the net.'

'So Mandelson's cash will be on a goalless draw?'

'And he'll get odds, spread a lot of small bets around …'

'Bastard,' Stevie said again. 'How did he get you into this, Matty?'

Matty shifted again. 'Something I did in London.'

'Secrets, eh? Hard things to keep.' Stevie got up, went to the mirror again, and just stood there, hands by his sides, staring into it. There was no emotion in his voice when he spoke.

'Tell him he can fuck himself.'

Matty had to choke out the words.

'You sure that's the message?'

'Cheerio, Matty.'

---

zappelte •

spielen im Moment nicht besonders gut •

du nicht dabei bist • würden sie auf wenig Widerstand stoßen • alle werden darauf wetten, dass du ein Tor schießt •

torlos

rutschte

wieder unruhig hin und her

er kann mich mal

• Die Worte blieben Matty fast im Hals stecken.

• Tschüs

Übung 51   Sind die folgenden Aussagen wahr oder falsch?
Tragen Sie ein T für true oder ein F für false in die Kästchen ein.

1.   Raith are having a lot of success at the moment.

2.   Nobody will be expecting Stevie to score a goal.

3.   Mr Mandelson will be betting on the match being a draw.

4.   Matty is being blackmailed because of something he did in Glasgow.

5.   Stevie is not interested in Mr Mandelson's offer.

6.   Stevie opens the door for Matty.

Matty rose shakily to his feet. 'What am I going to do?' — stand wacklig auf

'Cheerio, Matty.'

Stevie was as still as a statue as Matty walked to the door and let himself out. — hinausging

Mandelson sat at his desk, playing with a Cartier pen he'd taken from a punter that day. The man was overdue on a payment. The pen was by way of a gift. — Die Zahlung des Mannes war überfällig. • sollte ein Geschenk sein •

'So?' he asked Matty.

Matty sat on the chair and licked his lips. There was no offer of a drink today; this was just business. Malibu stood by the door. Matty took a deep breath – the last act of a drowning man. — holte tief Luft • Ertrinkender •

'It's on,' he said. — geht in Ordnung

Mandelson looked up at him. 'Stevie went for it?' — • hat sich bereit erklärt

'Eventually,' Matty said. 'You're sure?'

'As sure as I can be.'

'Well, that better be watertight, or you might find yourself going for a swim with heavy legs. Know what I mean?' — wasserdicht

Matty held the dark gaze and nodded. — Blick •

Mandelson glanced towards Malibu, both of them were smiling. Then he picked up the telephone. 'You know, — blickte flüchtig auf

7. Mr Mandelson had got the pen from a man who owed him money.
8. Malibu gets Matty something to drink.
9. Malibu stands by the window.
10. Matty tells Mr Mandelson that Stevie has rejected his offer.
11. Matty tells Mr Mandelson that it took him a long time to persuade Stevie to agree.
12. Malibu and Mr Mandelson are happy to hear Matty's news.

Matty,' he said, pushing numbers. 'I'm doing you a favour. You're doing *yourself* a favour.' He listened to the receiver. 'Mr Hamilton, please.' Then, to Matty, 'See, what you're doing here is saving your job. I overstretched myself, Matty. I wouldn't like that to get around, but I'm trusting you. If this comes off – and it better – then you've earned that trust.' He tapped the receiver. 'It wasn't all my own money either. But this will keep the Morvena alive and kicking.' He motioned for Matty to leave. Malibu tapped his shoulder as an incentive.

'Topper?' Mandelson was saying as Matty left the room. 'It's locked up. How much are you in for?'

Matty bided his time and waited till his shift was over. He walked out of the smart New Town building like a latterday Lazarus, and found the nearest payphone, then had to fumble through all the rubbish in his pockets, stuff that must have meant something once upon a time, until he found the card.

The card with a phone number on it.

The following Saturday, Stevie Scoular scored his team's only goal in their 1-0 win over Raith Rovers, and

Marginal glosses (left column):
während er
wählte •
Hörmuschel •
habe mich über-
nommen •
klappt • das
sollte es besser

gesund und
munter • als
Anreiz

Es ist unter
Dach und Fach.
Wie viel willst
du einsetzen? •
wartete die
Zeit ab •
der Gegenwart •
durchwühlen

Übung 52 Wenn ein Satz mehrere adverbiale Angaben hat, müssen sie eine bestimmte Reihenfolge haben. Im Deutschen ist die Reihenfolge temporal (zeitlich), modal (Art und Weise), lokal (örtlich), im Englischen dagegen modal, lokal, temporal. In den folgenden Sätzen stimmt die Reihenfolge der adverbialen Angaben nicht. Korrigieren Sie sie.

1. Mr Mandelson sat in his office alone this evening.
2. Rebus waited outside the door quietly.
3. Malibu went on Friday with a friend to the cinema.
4. Janis searched in her handbag frantically.

Mandelson sat alone in his office, his eyes on the Tele-text results.

His hand rested on the telephone receiver. He was expecting a call from Topper Hamilton. He couldn't seem to stop blinking, like there was a grain of sand in either eye. He buzzed the reception desk, told them to tell Malibu he was wanted. Mandelson didn't know how much time he had, but he knew he would make it count. A word with Stevie Scoular, see if Matty really *had* put the proposition to him. Then Matty himself … Matty was a definite, no matter what. Matty was about to be put out of the game.

The knock at the door had to be Malibu. Mandelson barked for him to come in. But when the door opened, two strangers sauntered in like they owned the place. Mandelson sat back in his chair, hands on the desk. He was almost relieved when they introduced themselves as police officers.

'I'm Detective Inspector Rebus,' the younger one said, 'this is Chief Superintendent Watson.'

'And you've come about the Benevolent Fund, right?' Rebus sat down unasked, his eyes drifting to the TV screen and the results posted there. 'Looks like you

Sandkorn •

rief … an

sie nutzen

ihm … den Vor-schlag gemacht hatte • war ein klarer Fall, ganz egal, was pas-sierte • schnauzte • schlenderten … herein

Unterstützungs-kasse • wander-ten • bekannt-gegeben

•

5. Stevie played on Saturday in Kirkcaldy.

6. Malibu waited in the car impatiently.

7. Brian saw Damon last week in Bowhill.

8. Rebus drives to Bowhill quickly.

9. Siobhan saw Rebus yesterday at the police station.

10. Malibu waits in the alley silently.

11. Rebus goes every night to the pub.

12. Rebus telephoned Brian last Friday from his office.

just lost a packet. I'm sorry to hear it. Did Topper take a beating, too?'

einen Haufen Geld • Hat es Topper auch erwischt?

Mandelson made fists of his hands. 'That wee bastard!'

Rebus was shaking his head. 'Matty did his best, only there was something he didn't know. Seems you didn't know either. Topper will be doubly disappointed.'

doppelt

'What?'

Farmer Watson, still standing, provided the answer. 'Ever heard of Big Ger Cafferty?'

Mandelson nodded. 'He's been in Barlinnie a while.'

'Used to be the biggest gangster on the east coast. Probably still is. And he's a fan of Stevie's, gets video-tapes of all his games. He almost sends him love letters.'

geschützt • Wenn Sie sich in seine Angelegenheiten einmischen, dann mischen Sie sich auch in Big Gers Angelegenheiten ein. • sein Mund wurde plötzlich trocken • hatte eine Scheißangst

Mandelson frowned. 'So?'

'So Stevie's covered,' Rebus said. 'Try fucking with him, you're asking Big Ger to bend over. Your little proposal has probably already made it back to Cafferty.'

Mandelson swallowed and felt suddenly dry-mouthed.

'There was no way Stevie was going to throw that game,' Rebus said quietly.

'Matty …' Mandelson choked the sentence off.

'Told you it was fixed? He was scared turdless, what

Übung 53 Setzen Sie die Verben in den folgenden Sätzen in die Zeitform, die in Klammern steht.

1. Rebus shakes his head. (Imperfekt)
2. Cafferty protects Stevie. (Futur)
3. Cafferty watches all of Stevie's matches. (Perfekt)
4. Cafferty is a fan of Stevie's. (Plusquamperfekt)
5. Rebus and Farmer Watson know all about Cafferty. (Imperfekt)
6. Matty played a trick on Mandelson. (Perfekt)
7. Matty belonged to Rebus. (Präsens)

else was he going to say? But Matty's *mine*. You don't touch him.'

'Not that you'd get the chance,' the Farmer added. 'Not with Topper *and* Cafferty after your blood. Malibu will be a big help, the way he took off five minutes ago in the Roller.' Watson walked up to the desk, looming over Mandelson like a mountain. 'You've got two choices, son. You can talk, or you can run.'

'You've got nothing.'

'I saw you that night at Gaitanos,' Rebus said. 'If you're going to lay out big bets, where better than Fife? Optimistic Raith fans might have bet on a goalless draw. You got Charmer Mackenzie to place the bets locally, spreading them around. That way it looked less suspicious.'

Which was why Mackenzie had wanted Rebus out of there, whatever the price: he'd been about to do some business ...

'Besides,' Rebus continued, 'when it comes down to it, what choice do you have?'

'You either talk to us ...' the Farmer said.

'Or you disappear. People do it all the time.'

And it never stops, Rebus could have added. Because

abgehauen ist •	
und ragte über	
... auf	
einsetzen	
und sie gut zu verteilen	
um jeden Preis	
außerdem •	
letzten Endes	

8. Malibu takes off in the Roller. (Perfekt)

9. Malibu is a big help. (Futur)

10. Rebus has seen Mandelson at Gaitanos. (Imperfekt)

11. Mandelson chose Fife for his bets. (Präsens)

12. Mackenzie does some business. (Plusquamperfekt)

13. Mandelson had only one choice. (Präsens)

14. Farmer Watson and Rebus give Mandelson a warning. (Imperfekt)

wechseln	it's part of the dance – shifting partners, people you shared the floor with, it all changed. And it only ended when you disappeared from the hall.
	And sometimes … sometimes, it didn't even end there.
mit leichenblassem Gesicht •	'All right,' Mandelson said at last, the way they'd known he would, all colour gone from his face, his
hohl •	voice hollow, 'what do you want to know?'
das … auswickelte	'Let's start with Topper Hamilton,' the Farmer said, sounding like a kid unwrapping his birthday present.

um zu wissen, woher er den Namen kannte	It was Wednesday morning when Rebus got the phone call from a Mr Bain. It took him a moment to place the name: Damon's bank manager.
• Bankfilialleiter	'Yes, Mr Bain, what can I do for you?'
	'Damon Mee, Inspector. You wanted us to keep an eye on any transactions.'
beugte sich … vor • Geldautomaten •	Rebus leaned forward in his chair. 'That's right.' 'There've been two withdrawals from cash machines, both in central London.'
griff nach	Rebus grabbed a pen. 'Where exactly?'
	'Tottenham Court Road was three days ago: fifty pounds. Next day, it was Finsbury Park, same amount.'

Übung 54   Vervollständigen Sie die Sätze mit den folgenden Wörtern.
(withdrawals, name, voice, eye, two, unwrapping, face)

1. All the colour has drained away from Mandelson's _____.

2. Mandelson's _____ sounds hollow.

3. Farmer Watson sounds like a kid _____ his birthday present.

4. It takes Rebus a moment to place Mr Bain's _____.

5. Rebus had asked Mr Bain to keep an _____ on Damon's bank account.

6. There have been two _____ from the account in London.

7. The withdrawal from Finsbury Park was made _____ days ago.

Fifty pounds a day: enough to live on, enough to pay for a cheap bed and breakfast* and two extra meals.

Frühstückspension • Konto

'How much is left in the account, Mr Bain?'

'A little under six hundred pounds.'

Enough for twelve days. There were several ways it could go. Damon could get himself a job. Or when the money ran out he could try begging. Or he could return home. Rebus thanked Bain and telephoned Janis.

ausging • zu betteln

'John,' she said, 'we got a postcard this morning.'

A postcard saying Damon was in London and doing fine. A postcard of apology for any fright he'd given them. A postcard saying he needed some time to 'get my head straight'. A postcard which ended 'See you soon.' The picture on the front was of a pair of breasts painted with Union Jacks.

als Entschuldigung • um meinen Kopf freizubekommen • britische Nationalflaggen

'Brian thinks we should go down there,' Janis said. 'Try to find him.'

Rebus thought of how many B&Bs there'd be in Finsbury Park. 'You might just chase him away,' he warned. 'He's doing OK, Janis.'

Frühstückspensionen • ihn ... verjagen

'But why did he do it, John? I mean, is it something *we* did?'

Bed and Breakfasts (auch einfach B&Bs genannt) findet man überall in Großbritannien. Normalerweise handelt es sich um eine Unterkunft bei Privatleuten, die im eigenen Haus Zimmer für Gäste bereitstellen. Dazu bekommt man ein English Breakfast, das aus Würstchen, Speck, Eiern, gebackenen Bohnen, Champignons, Toast und Tee oder Kaffee besteht. B&Bs sind eine günstige Übernachtungsmöglichkeit, wenn man eine Rundreise macht. In Städten kann ein B&B auch eine kleine Pension sein, die nur Zimmer mit Frühstück anbietet.

info

New questions and fears had replaced the old ones.
Rebus didn't know what to tell her. He wasn't family
and couldn't begin to answer her question. Didn't
want to begin to answer it.

'He's doing OK,' he repeated. 'Just give him some
time.'

She was crying now, softly. He imagined her with head
bowed, hair falling over the telephone receiver.

'We did everything, John. You can't know how much
we've given him. We always put ourselves second,
never a minute's thought for anything but him …'

'Janis …' he began.

She took a deep breath. 'Will you come and see me,
John?'

Rebus looked around the office, eyes resting eventually on his own desk and the paperwork stacked there.
'I can't, Janis. I'd like to, but I just can't. See, it's not as
if I…'

He didn't know how he was going to finish the sentence, but it didn't matter. She'd put her phone down.
He sat back in his chair and remembered dancing with
her, how brittle her body had seemed. But that had
been half a lifetime ago. They'd made so many choices

Margin glosses:
ersetzt •
gehörte nicht zur Familie
mit gesenktem Kopf
er hat bei uns immer an erster Stelle gestanden
blieben … hängen • der dort aufgestapelten Schreibarbeit
aufgelegt
zerbrechlich

Übung 55 Beantworten Sie die Fragen zum Text.
Welche Lösung ist die richtige?

1. How does Rebus imagine Janis as he talks to her on the phone?
  a) Lying in the garden.
  b) Cooking the evening meal.
  c) Crying with her head bowed.

2. What does Rebus see piled up on his desk?
  a) Old magazines.
  b) His paperwork.
  c) Lots of dictionaries.

since. It was time to let the past go. Siobhan Clarke was at her desk. She was looking at him. Then she mimed the drinking of a cup of coffee, and he nodded and got to his feet.

Did a little dance as he shuffled towards her.

stellte ... pantomimisch dar

3. What does Siobhan mime to Rebus?
   a) Having a cup of coffee.
   b) Doing paperwork.
   c) Doing a dance.

4. What does Rebus do as he approaches Siobhan?
   a) He falls over.
   b) He does a little dance.
   c) He puts on his coat.

No Sanity Clause
AN INSPECTOR REBUS STORY FOR CHRISTMAS

It was all Edgar Allan Poe's fault. Either that or the Scottish Parliament*. Joey Briggs was spending most of his days in the run-up to Christmas sheltering from Edinburgh's biting December winds. He'd been walking up George IV Bridge one day and had watched a down-and-out slouching into the Central Library. Joey had hesitated. He wasn't a down-and-out, not yet anyway. Maybe he would be soon, if Scully Aitchison MSP* got his way, but for now Joey had a bedsit and a trickle of state cash. Thing was, nothing made you miss money more than Christmas. The shop windows displayed their magnetic pull. There were queues at the cash machines. Kids tugged on their parents' sleeves, ready with something new to add to the present list. Boyfriends were out buying gold, while families piled

Zurechnungs-
fähigkeitsklausel
(Wortspiel mit
Santa Claus;
Titel eines
Punk-Songs) •
Vorweihnachts-
zeit • indem er
sich ... unter-
stellte • schnei-
dend • Penner
• der ... latschte
• Mitglied des
schottischen
Parlaments •
möbliertes
Zimmer • Geld •
Anziehungskraft
• zogen heftig

info

Nach dem Act of Union (Vereinigungsgesetz) 1707, das die Königreiche England und Schottland vereinigte, gab es in Schottland kein eigenständiges Parlament mehr. Erst 1997, als Tony Blairs Labour Party, die die Dezentralisierung unterstützte, die Wahl gewann, wurde ein Referendum über ein schottisches Parlament abgehalten. Das neue Parlament konstituierte sich am 12. Mai 1999. Das schottische Parlament besteht aus 129 Abgeordneten oder MSPs und wird von einem First Minister (Ministerpräsidenten) geleitet. Es hat die Entscheidungsgewalt in Bildung, Justiz, Landwirtschaft und Gesundheit. Außerdem kann es den Steuersatz ändern.

the food trolley high. And then there was Joey, nine weeks out of prison and nobody to call his friend. He knew there was nothing waiting for him back in his home town. His wife had taken the children and tiptoed out of his life. Joey's sister had written to him in prison with the news. So, eleven months on, Joey had walked through the gates of Saughton Jail and taken the first bus into the city centre, purchased an evening paper and started the hunt for somewhere to live.

The bedsit was fine. It was one of four in a tenement basement just off South Clerk Street, sharing a kitchen and bathroom. The other men worked, didn't say much. Joey's room had a gas fire with a coin-meter beside it, too expensive to keep it going all day. He'd tried sitting in the kitchen with the stove lit, until the landlord had caught him. Then he'd tried steeping in the bath, topping up the hot. But the water always seemed to run cold after half a tub.

'You could try getting a job,' the landlord had said.

Not so easy with a prison record. Most of the jobs were for security and nightwatch. Joey didn't think he'd get very far there. Following the tramp into the library

Margin glossary (left column):
- Einkaufswagen
- sich aus …
- gestohlen •
- später •
- (Gefängnis in Edinburgh) •
- gekauft •
- Souterrain eines Mietshauses • in einer Querstraße zur • Heizgerät •
- Münzzähler •
- Herd • Vermieter • sich … einzuweichen • indem er … nachfüllte • wenn die Wanne halbvoll war •
- Wachpersonal •
- Nachtwache •
- Penner

Übung 56 Die folgenden Sätze enthalten jeweils einen grammatischen Fehler. Suchen und korrigieren Sie ihn.

1. Joey knows there's nothing to wait for him in his home town.

2. Joey's sister had wrote to him in prison.

3. The news about his wife are bad.

4. Joey had to look after a place to live.

5. The landlord had catched Joey using the stove as a heater.

6. Joey had tried steep in the bath.

was one of his better ideas. The uniform behind the desk gave him a look, but didn't say anything. Joey wandered the stacks, picked out a book and sat himself down. And that was that. He became a regular, the staff acknowledged him with a nod and sometimes even a smile. He kept himself presentable, didn't fall asleep the way some of the old guys did. He read for much of the day, alternating between fiction, biographies and textbooks. He read up on local history, plumbing and Winston Churchill, Nigel Tranter's novels and National Trust gardens. He knew the library would close over Christmas, didn't know what he'd do without it. He never borrowed books, because he was afraid they'd have him on some blacklist: convicted housebreaker and petty thief, not to be trusted with loan material. He dreamt of spending Christmas in one of the town's posh hotels, looking out across Princes Street Gardens* to the Castle. He'd order room service and watch TV. He'd take as many baths as he liked. They'd clean his clothes for him and return them to the room. He dreamt of the presents he'd buy himself: a big radio with a CD player, some new shirts and pairs of shoes; and books. Plenty of books.

Regale • wählte
... aus • Personal
• nickte ihm zu

wechselte zwischen • Romane • Lehrbücher • las sich in ... ein • Klempnerarbeiten • lieh ... aus • verurteilter Einbrecher • kleiner Dieb • Material zum Ausleihen • vornehm • Zimmerservice

Der Park Princes Street Gardens liegt im Tal zwischen der Princes Street, der Haupteinkaufstraße Edinburghs, und dem erloschenen Vulkan, auf dem die Burg erbaut wurde. Auf alten Gemälden kann man erkennen, dass der Park einst ein See, der Nor Loch, war, der die Burg umringte. Im frühen neunzehnten Jahrhundert wurde der See aus Gesundheitsgründen trockengelegt und ein öffentlicher Park angelegt. Der Park ist anderthalb Kilometer lang und bietet im Sommer viel Platz zum Picknicken. Im Winter befinden sich dort eine Eisbahn und ein deutscher Weihnachtsmarkt.

info

The dream became almost real to him, so that he found himself nodding off in the library, coming to as his head hit the page he'd been reading. Then he'd have to concentrate, only to find himself drifting into a warm sleep again.

eingenickt • und aufwachte

Until he met Edgar Allan Poe.

It was a book of poems and short stories, among them 'The Purloined Letter'. Joey loved that, thought it was really clever the way you could hide something by putting it right in front of people. Something that didn't look out of place, people would just ignore it. There'd been a guy in Saughton, doing time for fraud. He'd told Joey: 'Three things: a suit, a haircut and an expensive watch. If you've got those, it's amazing what you can get away with.' He'd meant that clients had trusted him, because they'd seen something they were comfortable with, something they expected to see. What they hadn't seen was what was right in front of their noses, to wit: a shark, someone who was going to take a big bite out of their savings.

gestohlen

fehl am Platz •

er saß wegen Betrugs •

was man sich alles erlauben kann

nämlich • Hai

As Joey's eyes flitted back over Poe's story, he started to get an idea. He started to get what he thought was a very good idea indeed. Problem was, he needed what

als Joey wieder Poes Geschichte überflog

Übung 57   Beantworten Sie die Fragen zum Text.

1. What does Joey nearly do in the library?
2. What causes him to wake up?
3. What does Joey particularly like about 'The Purloined Letter' story?
4. What crime had the other man in Saughton committed?
5. What are the three things you need to get people to trust you, according to the man in Saughton?
6. What had the man in Saughton meant by 'the start-up'?

the fraudster had called 'the start-up', meaning some cash. He happened to look across to where one of the old tramps was slumped on a chair, the newspaper in front of him unopened. Joey looked around: nobody was watching. The place was dead: who had time to go to the library when Christmas was around the corner? Joey walked over to the old guy, slipped a hand into his coat pocket. Felt coins and notes, bunched his fingers around them. He glanced down at the newspaper. There was a story about Scully Aitchison's campaign. Aitchison was the MSP who wanted all offenders put on a central register, open to public inspection. He said law-abiding folk had the right to know if their neighbour was a thief or a murderer – as if stealing was the same as killing somebody! There was a small photo of Aitchison, too, beaming that self-satisfied smile, his glasses glinting. If Aitchison got his way, Joey would never get out of the rut. Not unless his plan paid off.

John Rebus saw his girlfriend kissing Santa Claus. There was a German Market in Princes Street Gardens. That was where Rebus was to meet Jean. He hadn't expected to find her in a clinch with a man dressed

Betrüger	
zusammenge-sackt • verlassen	
steckte … heim-lich • krallte sie	
Straftäter • Prüfung • gesetzestreu	
selbstgefällig • funkelnd • aus dem Trott herauskommen • gelang	
von einem Mann umarmt	

7. What did the old tramp have in front of him?
8. Why is the library so quiet?
9. What does Joey find in the tramp's pocket?
10. What is Scully Aitchison campaigning for?
11. If Scully Aitchison's campaign succeeds, what effect will this have on Joey's situation?
12. What is Jean doing when Rebus sees her in Princes Street Gardens?

machte sich los

• erschallten •

überrascht

in a red suit, black boots and snowy-white beard.
Santa broke away and moved off, just as Rebus was
approaching. German folk songs were blaring out.
There was a startled look on Jean's face.

'What was that all about?' he asked.

'I don't know.' She was watching the retreating figure.
'I think maybe he's just had too much festive spirit. He

feierlich gestimmt

(Wortspiel, spirit

= Spirituosen/

Stimmung) •

tätlicher Angriff

• ihre Selbstbe-

herrschung

wiederfindend •

Wache

came up and grabbed me.' Rebus made to follow, but
Jean stopped him. 'Come on, John. Season of goodwill
and all that.'

'It's assault, Jean.'

She laughed, regaining her composure. 'You're going
to take St Nicholas down the station and put him in
the cells?' She rubbed his arm. 'Let's forget it, eh? The
fun starts in ten minutes.'

Rebus wasn't too sure that the evening was going to be

mit ... über-

schüttet •

Erleichterung

'fun'. He spent every day bogged down in crimes and
tragedies. He wasn't sure that a 'mystery dinner' was
going to offer much relief. It had been Jean's idea.
There was a hotel just across the road. You all went in
for dinner, were handed envelopes telling you which
character you'd be playing. A body was discovered, and
then you all turned detective.

Übung 58   Die folgenden Sätze enthalten jeweils einen grammatischen Fehler.
Suchen und korrigieren Sie ihn.

1. Santa moved off just as Rebus were approaching.

2. Jean has a startled look in her face.

3. Jean thinks that the man dressed as Santa Claus has having
too much to drink.

4. Jean asks Rebus if he's really going arrest Santa Claus.

5. Rebus isn't looking forward at the evening.

'It'll be fun,' Jean insisted, leading him out of the gardens. She had three shopping bags with her. He wondered if any of them were for him. She'd asked for a list of his Christmas wants, but so far all he'd come up with were a couple of CDs by String Driven Thing.

As they entered the hotel, they saw that the mystery evening was being held on the mezzanine floor. Most of the guests had already gathered and were enjoying glasses of cava. Rebus asked in vain for a beer.

'Cava's included in the price,' the waitress told him. A man dressed in Victorian costume was checking names and handing out carrier bags.

'Inside,' he told Jean and Rebus, 'you'll find instructions, a secret clue that only you know, your name, and an item of clothing.'

'Oh,' Jean said, 'I'm Little Nell*.' She fixed a bonnet to her head. 'Who are you, John?'

'Mr Bumble*.' Rebus produced his name-tag and a yellow woollen scarf, which Jean insisted on tying around his neck.

'It's a Dickensian* theme, specially for Christmas,' the host revealed, before moving off to confront his other victims. Everyone looked a bit embarrassed, but most

beharrte	
Wünsche • was ihm eingefallen war •	
Zwischengeschoss •	
Sekt • umsonst	
viktorianisch • Plastiktüten	
Hinweis	
Haube	
Namensschild	
Dickens'sches • Gastgeber • gegenüberzutreten	

Charles Dickens war ein englischer Schriftsteller des neunzehnten Jahrhunderts. Seine ersten Romane wurden als Fortsetzungsgeschichten in Zeitungen veröffentlicht, und er wurde durch seine scharfe Beobachtungsgabe und seine unvergesslichen Figuren mit ihren wunderbaren Namen zum beliebtesten Schriftsteller des Landes. Er interessierte sich besonders für das Leben der unteren Klassen, und seine Bücher enthalten oft Kritik an der viktorianischen Gesellschaft. Die Figuren, die Rebus und Jean spielen, kommen aus seinen Romanen **The Old Curiosity Shop** (Little Nell) und **Oliver Twist** (Mr Bumble).

info

were trying for enthusiasm. Rebus didn't doubt that a couple of glasses of wine over dinner would loosen a few Edinburgh stays. There were a couple of faces he recognised. One was a journalist, her arm around her boyfriend's waist. The other was a man who appeared to be with his wife. He had one of those looks to him, the kind that says you should know him. She was blonde and petite and about a decade younger than her husband.

'Isn't that an MSP?' Jean whispered.

'His name's Scully Aitchison,' Rebus told her.

Jean was reading her information sheet. 'The victim tonight is a certain Ebenezer Scrooge,' he said.

'And did you kill him?'

She thumped his arm. Rebus smiled, but his eyes were on the MSP. Aitchison's face was bright red. Rebus guessed he'd been drinking since lunchtime. His voice boomed across the floor, broadcasting the news that he and Catriona had booked a room for the night, so they wouldn't have to drive back to the constituency. They were all mingling on the mezzanine landing. The room where they'd dine was just off to the right, its doors still closed. Guests were starting to ask each

Margin glossary:
lockern • Korsette
Jahrzehnt
Sie versetzte ihm einen Schlag am Arm. • dröhnte • die Nachricht verbreitend • Wahlkreis • mischten sich • Flur • essen

Übung 59   Die folgende Zusammenfassung des Textes auf diesen Seiten enthält sechs sachliche Fehler. Können Sie sie finden und korrigieren?

Rebus thinks that people will start to relax once they have had a few drinks. He recognises a few of the party guests. One is a journalist and one is a man who he thinks he knows who is here with his older wife. Jean thinks he's an MSP and Rebus confirms that it's Scully Aitchison. Jean says that, according to the information sheet, the murderer is called Ebenezer Scrooge. Rebus guesses that Aitchison has had a lot to drink. Aitchison announces to everyone that he and his wife have booked a hotel room for the

other which characters they were playing. As one eld- | einen Mann in
erly lady – Miss Havisham on her name-tag – came | einem roten
over to ask Jean about Little Nell, Rebus saw a red-suit- | Anzug
ed man appear at the top of the stairs. Santa carried
what looked like a half-empty sack. He started making
his way across the floor, but was stopped by Aitchison.
'*J'accuse!*' the MSP bawled. 'You killed Scrooge | Sie sind schuldig!
because of his inhumanity to his fellow man!' Aitchi- | • brüllte • Un-
son's wife came to the rescue, dragging her husband | menschlichkeit •
away, but Santa's eyes seemed to follow them. As he | Mitmensch
made to pass Rebus, Rebus fixed him with a stare.
'Jean,' he asked, 'is he the same one …?'
She only caught the back of Santa's head. 'They all
look alike to me,' she said.
Santa was on his way to the next flight of stairs. Rebus | Treppe
watched him leave, then turned back to the other
guests, all of them now tricked out in odd items of | geschmückt mit
clothing. No wonder Santa had looked like he'd stum- | • als wäre er
bled into an asylum. Rebus was reminded of a Marx | aus Versehen in
Brothers line, Groucho trying to get Chico's name on a | eine Irrenanstalt
contract, telling him to sign the sanity clause. | eingetreten •
But, as Chico said, everyone knew there was no such | Witz
thing as Sanity Clause.

week. Whilst a young lady asks Jean about Little Nell, Rebus
spots a man dressed as Santa Claus at the top of the stairs. As he
tries to cross the room, Aitchison accuses the man of being the
murderer. He gives Scrooge's inhumanity to his fellow man as the
reason for the crime. His wife drags him away. Rebus stares at
the man dressed as Santa and asks Jean if it's the same one that
gave her a hug in the park. Jean is sure it is. Rebus watches Santa
leave the room and turns back to the other guests. Everyone is
now wearing a mask to represent their character from Dickens.

Joey jimmied open his third room of the night. The Santa suit had worked a treat. Okay, so it was hot and uncomfortable, and the beard was itching his neck, but it worked! He'd breezed through reception and up the stairs. So far, as he'd worked the corridors all he'd had were a few jokey comments. No one from security asking him who he was. No guests becoming suspicious. He fitted right in, and he was right under their noses. God bless Edgar Allan Poe.

The woman in the fancy dress shop had even thrown in a sack, saying he'd be wanting to fill it. How true: in the first bedroom, he'd dumped out the crumpled sheets of old newspaper and started filling the sack – clothes, jewellery, the contents of the mini-bar. Same with the second room: a tap on the door to make sure no one was home, then the chisel into the lock and hey presto. Thing was, there wasn't much in the rooms. A notice in the wardrobe told clients to lock all valuables in the hotel safe at reception. Still, he had a few nice things: camera, credit cards, bracelet and necklace. Sweat was running into his eyes, but he couldn't afford to shed his disguise. He was starting to have crazy thoughts: take a good long soak; ring down for room service; find a

Margin notes (left column):

stemmte ... auf • war ein Riesenerfolg gewesen • war ohne Schwierigkeiten durch ... gekommen • scherzhaft

Kostümladen • extra dazugegeben • weggeschmissen

Meißel • Simsalabim • Wertsachen

seine Verkleidung abzulegen • ein langes Bad zu nehmen

Übung 60 Ordnen Sie den folgenden Wörtern aus dem Text die passende deutsche Übersetzung zu.

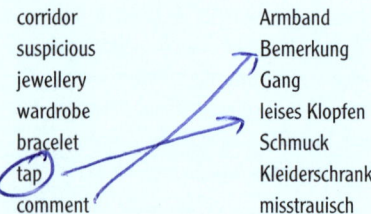

corridor	Armband
suspicious	Bemerkung
jewellery	Gang
wardrobe	leises Klopfen
bracelet	Schmuck
tap	Kleiderschrank
comment	misstrauisch

room that hadn't been taken and settle in for the duration. In the third room, he sat on the bed, feeling dizzy. There was a briefcase open beside him, just lots of paperwork. His stomach growled, and he remembered that his last meal had been a Mars Bar supper the previous day. He broke open a jar of salted peanuts, switched the TV on while he ate. As he put the empty jar down, he happened to glance at the contents of the briefcase. 'Parliamentary briefing … Law and Justice Sub-Committee …' He saw a list of names on the top sheet. One of them was coloured with a yellow marker.

Scully Aitchison.

The drunk man downstairs … That was where Joey knew him from! He leapt to his feet, trying to think. He could stay here and give the MSP a good hiding. He could … He picked up the room-service menu, called down and ordered smoked salmon, a steak, a bottle each of best red wine and malt whisky. Then heard himself saying those sweetest words: 'Put it on my room, will you?'

Then he settled back to wait. Flipped through the paperwork again. An envelope slipped out. Card inside, and a letter inside the card.

es sich für diese Zeit gemütlich zu machen • knurrte	
Unterausschuss	
Leuchtstift	
dem MSP eine ordentliche Tracht Prügel verpassen	
Setzen Sie es auf meine Zimmerrechnung. • blätterte … durch	

Dear Scully, it began. *I hope it isn't all my fault, this idea of yours for a register of offenders…*

'I haven't a clue,' said Rebus.

Nor did he. Dinner was over, the actor playing Scrooge was flat out on the mezzanine floor, and Rebus was as far away from solving the crime as ever. Thankfully, a bar had been opened up, and he spent most of his time perched on a high stool, pretending to read the background notes while taking sips of beer. Jean had hooked up with Miss Havisham, while Aitchison's wife was slumped in one of the armchairs, drawing on a cigarette. The MSP himself was playing ringmaster, and had twice confronted Rebus, calling for him to reveal himself as the villain.

'Innocent, m'lud,' was all Rebus had said.

'We think it's Magwitch,' Jean said, suddenly breathless by Rebus's side, her bonnet at a jaunty angle. 'He and Scrooge knew one another in prison.'

'I didn't know Scrooge served time,' Rebus said.

'That's because you're not asking questions.'

'I don't need to; I've got you to tell me. That's what makes a good detective.'

Margin glosses: keine Ahnung • ausgestreckt • sitzend • an seinem Bier nippte • hatte sich … angeschlossen • Zirkusdirektor • sich als der Übeltäter zu erkennen zu geben • Euer Gnaden • schief aufgesetzt • im Gefängnis saß

Übung 61 Sind die folgenden Aussagen wahr oder falsch?
Tragen Sie ein T für true oder ein F für false in die Kästchen ein.

1. The actor playing Scrooge is lying on the floor.
2. Rebus thinks he has already solved the crime.
3. Rebus sits at the bar drinking wine.
4. Jean is talking to Aitchison's wife.
5. Aitchison thinks Rebus is the murderer.
6. Some of the diners have started questioning Magwitch.

He watched her march away. Four of the diners had
encircled the poor man playing Magwitch. Rebus had
harboured suspicions, too … but now he was thinking
of jail time, and how it affected those serving it. It gave
them a certain look, a look they brought back into the
world on their release. The same look he'd seen in
Santa's eyes.

Gäste •
umringt • hatte
… den Verdacht
gehabt • die im
Gefängnis saßen
• wenn sie ent-
lassen wurden

And here was Santa now, coming back down the stairs,
his sack slung over one shoulder. Crossing the mezzanine floor as if seeking someone out. Then finding
them: Scully Aitchison. Rebus rose from his stool and
wandered over. 'Have you been good this year?' Santa
was asking Aitchison.

über eine Schul-
ter geschmissen

ging hinüber

'No worse than anyone else,' the MSP smirked.

grinste

'Sure about that?' Santa's eyes narrowed.

'I wouldn't lie to Father Christmas.'

'What about this plan of yours, the offender register?'

Aitchison blinked a couple of times. 'What about it?'

Santa held a piece of paper aloft, his voice rising. 'Your
own nephew's serving time for fraud. Managed to keep
that quiet, haven't you?'

in die Höhe

betrug

Aitchison stared at the letter. 'Where in hell …?'
How …?'

7. Rebus has seen the look of a released prisoner
   in Miss Havisham's eyes.
8. Santa appears, dragging his sack behind him.
9. Santa is looking for Rebus.
10. Aitchison claims he wouldn't lie to Santa Claus.
11. Santa asks Aitchison about his plan for an offender register.
12. Aitchison's nephew is in prison for armed robbery.

The journalist stepped forward. 'Mind if I take a look?'
Santa handed over the letter, then pulled off his hat and beard. Started heading for the stairs down. Rebus blocked his way.

übergab

versperrte ihm den Weg

'Time to hand out the presents,' he said quietly. Joey looked at him and understood immediately, slid the sack from his shoulder. Rebus took it. 'Now on you go.'
'You're not arresting me?'
'Who'd feed Dancer* and Prancer*?' Rebus asked.
His stomach full of steak and wine, a bottle of malt in the capacious pocket of his costume, Joey smiled his way back towards the outside world.

Malt Whisky •
geräumig

info

In der anglo-amerikanischen Weihnachtstradition wird der Schlitten des Weihnachtsmanns von acht oder neun Rentieren durch die Luft gezogen. Die Namen dieser Rentiere erschienen zum ersten Mal in dem Gedicht A Visit from St Nicholas aus dem Jahre 1823. Sie heißen Dasher, Dancer, Prancer, Vixen, Comet, Cupid, Donner und Blitzen. Später kam Rudolph mit der roten Nase (Rudolph the red-nosed Reindeer) auch dazu. Es ist in Großbritannien und den USA üblich, an Heiligabend eine Stärkung für den Weihnachtsmann im Wohnzimmer oder am Ende des Betts zu hinterlassen. Dazu kommen einige Möhren für die Rentiere.

Lösungen

1　**1.** die Gabe, die es ermöglicht, sich an Dinge zu erinnern: **memory** (Gedächtnis)
　　2. eine Statue oder ein Denkmal, das die Menschen an ein Ereignis oder
　　　　eine berühmte Persönlichkeit erinnern soll: **memorial** (Denkmal)
　　3. etwas, das man kauft oder aufbewahrt, um sich an ein bestimmtes Ereignis zu
　　　　erinnern: **memento** (Andenken)
　　4. mit kurzen, langsamen, schleppenden Schritten gehen: **to shuffle** (schlurfen)
　　5. sich mit kurzen, abgehackten Bewegungen schnell bewegen: **to dart around**
　　　　(umherhuschen)
　　6. suchen: **to seek out** (suchen)

2　**1.** 〔F〕 Die Gasse hinter dem Guisers war leer.
　　2. 〔F〕 Der Besitzer des Mercedes war sehr besorgt um die Person, die
　　　　niedergestochen worden war.
　　3. 〔T〕 **Die meisten Besucher des Gaitanos hatten den Club in Guisers**
　　　　umbenannt.
　　4. 〔T〕 **Der Club wird erst am späten Abend voll.**
　　5. 〔F〕 Dem Fachmann für Veranstaltungstechnik waren seine Rülpser sehr peinlich.

3　Rebus and the technician are watching the security video from the nightclub.
　　The quality of the tape **is very bad**. The tape shows the back alley, then the dance
　　floor and then the main bar where there are **a lot of** people waiting to be served.
　　Rebus gets closer to the screen and compares the image of a man with **a number of**
　　photographs which he has brought with him. He thinks he has identified the man.

4　**Richtig:** stunning (atemberaubend), distracted (geistesabwesend)

　　Falsch: bald (kahlköpfig), unattractive (wenig anziehend), straight-haired (mit
　　　　　　glatten Haaren), warmly-dressed (warm angezogen), talkative (gesprächig)

5　**1.** He took two buses.
　　2. The trips to the football were intended to fill the gap left by their mother's death.
　　3. Nothing. He stared at him in silence.
　　4. Yes, sometimes he drifts off to a pleasant place in his mind.

6　**1.** Rebus's boss put his head ~~over~~ **round** the door.
　　2. The Farmer ~~were~~ **was** pouring a mug of coffee.
　　3. The Farmer offered Rebus some coffee, but he turned ~~up~~ **down** the offer.
　　4. The Farmer told Rebus that it ~~will~~ **would** soon be his birthday.
　　5. The Farmer folded ~~the~~ **his** arms.

7 **1.** remembering (erinnerte sich an) = thinking back
   2. to go to court (vor Gericht gehen) = to proceed to trial
   3. thinner (dünner) = more slender
   4. solved a dispute (schlichtete einen Streit) = settled an argument
   5. was still not satisfied (war noch nicht zufrieden) = wasn't yet content

8 **1.** The Farmer wants to get Topper in **court**.
   2. It isn't against the law to **invest** in a casino.
   3. Topper's name didn't **come up** during the vetting procedure.
   4. Rebus's snitch works as a **croupier**.
   5. Rebus made his snitch a **promise**.
   6. Rebus's snitch won't give him information on the **management**.

9 The Farmer asked if this was suspicious. Rebus shrugged and said that it could be and that he had gone up to the bar for a round of drinks and never come back. The Farmer pointed out that everyone had done that in their time. Rebus said that his parents were worried. The Farmer asked how old he was and Rebus replied that he was twenty-three. The Farmer thought about this and then asked what the problem was.

10 **1.** Eine kleinwüchsige, aber sehr harte Person: terrier
   2. Etwas geräuschvoll zwischen den Zähnen zermalmen: to crunch (knirschend zerkauen)
   3. Ein Buch, das für den Unterricht in einem Fach bestimmt ist: textbook (Lehrbuch)
   4. Aufgeregt und energisch werden: to fizz (sprudeln)
   5. von geringer Wichtigkeit: minor (geringfügig)
   6. Gebiet: territory (Territorium)

11 **1.** b) Sie holte ein paar Erkundigungen ein.
   2. a) Sie stritten sich nie.
   3. c) Wenn Damons Leiche gefunden wurde.
   4. b) Sein Bruder.

12 **1.** To outsiders the place **means** coastal scenery.
   2. The west-central Fife of Rebus's childhood **was** very different.
   3. They **are building** new roads.
   4. The place **won't** feel so very different.
   5. Locals still **know** it as a village distinct from its neighbour.

13 **1.** Rebus had been brought ~~round~~ **up** in a similar house to Brian's.
   2. Brian ~~practical~~ **practically** opened the car door for Rebus.
   3. Brian was trying to shake ~~the~~ **his** hand while Rebus was still emerging from his seat.
   4. Rebus was guided to the seat ~~on~~ **by** the fire.
   5. Janis tells Rebus that Damon is saving up to ~~become~~ **get** married.
   6. The date of the wedding is set ~~on~~ **for** next August.

14 1. T Das erste Foto, das Rebus sieht, zeigt Damon kurz nachdem er von der Schule abgegangen ist.
2. T Rebus ist froh, dass er die Gesichter der anderen Menschen um ihn herum nicht ansehen muss.
3. F Damon war allein mit seinen Eltern im Urlaub in Lanzarote.
4. T Rebus findet, dass Janis im Bikini gut aussieht.
5. T Rebus will ein paar Fotos von Damon behalten.
6. F Helen wohnt am anderen Ende der Stadt.
7. F Herr Playfair bietet an, Helen anzurufen.
8. F Das Guisers befindet sich an der Strandpromenade in Kirkcaldy.
9. F Das Gebäude, in dem sich das Guisers befindet, war schon immer ein Nachtclub.
10. T Damon und sein Vater arbeiten bei derselben Firma.
11. T Damons Vater nutzte seine Beziehungen, um seinem Sohn eine Stelle zu besorgen.
12. F Frau Playfair ist verärgert, weil Rebus den ganzen Kuchen gegessen hat.

15 Sieben Verben stehen im Plusquamperfekt: hadn't been able to, hadn't been there, he'd vanished, she'd introduced him, someone who had, Andy had been part, there'd been four of them.
Helen Cousins wasn't able to add much to Rebus's picture of Damon, and wasn't there the night he vanished. But she introduced him to someone who was, Andy Peters. Andy was part of the group at Gaitanos. There were four of them.

16 The bank manager tells Rebus that Damon withdrew one hundred pounds from his account in Kirkcaldy on the twenty-second but that he did not know the exact time of the transaction. The information is very up-to-date. Rebus asks the manager to keep an eye on the account and let him know if anyone uses it again. The manager is unwilling to do this without a written request and possibly Head Office approval. Later Rebus receives a call from DS Hendry about the Gaitanos club.

17 1. Eine enge Straße hinter oder zwischen Gebäuden: alley (Gasse)
2. Eine Person, die an einem bestimmten Ort wohnt: resident (Ortsansässiger)
3. Nichts Illegales getan haben: to be clean (sauber sein)
4. Etwas, mit dem man sich zuallererst beschäftigen soll: priority (Wichtigkeit)
5. Richtig oder legal: rightful (rechtmäßig)

18 brave, braver, bravest
good, better, best
boring, more boring, most boring
hot, hotter, hottest
tiny, tinier, tiniest
horrible, more horrible, most horrible
cheap, cheaper, cheapest
bad, worse, worst

19
bet	Wette
surveillance	Überwachung
trainee	Auszubildender
flaw	Fehler
to vary	ändern
select	erlesen
master	beherrschen

20 **1.** Most houses like the fact that Matty is **flexible**.
   2. Matty's latest employers seem **laid back**.
   3. Husbands and wives coming in is proof of a **relaxed atmosphere**.
   4. A lot of the younger punters are **Asian**.
   5. The day boss thinks the Asians keep their money in their **underwear**.
   6. The Asians wear **crumpled** jackets and shirts.

21 **1.** **She** wrote **it** for **him**.
   2. **He** didn't approve of **them**.
   3. **It** is next door to **it**.
   4. **He** used to go out with **her**.
   5. **She** is now married to **him**.

22 **Richtig:** smartly-dressed (schick angezogen), famous (berühmt), friendly (freundlich)

   Falsch: penniless (arm), ugly (hässlich), ancient (uralt), arrogant (überheblich)

23 **Richtig:** dark-haired (dunkelhaarig), middle-aged (im mittleren Alter), scarred (narbig)

   Falsch: bald (kahlköpfig), blond (blond), young (jung), puny (schwächlich)

24 **1.** **b)** Einige alkoholische und alkoholfreie Getränke.
   2. **c)** Solange er noch Tore schießt.
   3. **a)** Ein paar Tage.
   4. **c)** Einen Video-Fachmann und einen besseren Videorekorder.

25 **1.** Rebus was ~~worked~~ **working** the case in his free time.
   2. No money had been withdrawn ~~out of~~ **from** the cash machine.
   3. No money had been taken from ~~those~~ **that** account.
   4. Sometimes runaways want to shed ~~the~~ **their** whole identity.
   5. Rebus checks with a colleague that he had done all that he ~~can~~ **could**.
   6. The problem is like looking ~~at a~~ **for** a needle in a haystack.

26 Rebus's colleague tells him that there are approximately 25,000 missing persons a year **which are reported**. Rebus then phones Janis and suggests to her that she might produce some **flyers** which she could hang up around town and hand out to people. She should include a photo of Damon with a physical description of him and what he was wearing that night. When she starts crying, Rebus asks her if she'd like him **to drop by**.

27 **1.** swapped (tauschten) = exchanged
   2. blow (Schlag) = punch
   3. annoyed (verärgert) = angry
   4. to say sorry (sich entschuldigen) = to apologise
   5. vacation (Ferien) = holidays
   6. serious (ernst) = solemn

28   **1.** F Rebus nähert sich Janis, als sich die Haustür öffnet.
    2. T Janis' und Brians Haus ist immer voller Besucher.
    3. T Janis umarmt ihre Mutter zur Begrüßung.
    4. F Rebus verabschiedet sich, als er die zwei Frauen verlässt.
    5. T Rebus spricht im Nachtclub mit einem der Türsteher.
    6. F Die Videokamera funktioniert offensichtlich nicht.
    7. F Rebus und Charles Mackenzie haben sich noch nie vorher gesprochen.
    8. T Herr Mackenzie ist sehr klein und dünn, und seine Haare werden grau.
    9. T Herr Mackenzie betritt das Büro vor Rebus.
   10. T Im Büro befindet sich auch Putzzeug.

29 **1.** I parked my Mercedes in the alley.
   2. Do you want your video back?
   3. We enhanced the photograph on our computer.
   4. Rebus is standing in his office.
   5. He is helping Janis and Brian to find their son.
   6. Is that man her boyfriend?

30 frown   die Stirn runzeln
   continue   fortfahren
   palm   Handfläche
   thoughtless   rücksichtslos
   assistance   Hilfe
   ambience   Atmosphäre

31   **1.** Mr Mackenzie keeps his money in his desk drawer.
    2. Mr Mackenzie offers Rebus one hundred pounds.
    3. Mr Mackenzie's offer of money makes Rebus stay at the club.
    4. No, none of the staff at the club recognises the woman in the photo.
    5. Two male customers recognise the woman in the photo.
    6. The lads think the woman in the photo is a cracker.
    7. The two men have seen the woman in the photo at the club only once.
    8. They have no idea if she was alone at the club.
    9. They don't recognise Damon from the photo because they don't pay attention to the men at the club.
   10. The bass makes Rebus feel queasy.
   11. Rebus thinks the woman in the photo might have been speaking to Damon because of the way her head is angled and because her mouth is open.
   12. Damon's friends are sure that he didn't talk to the woman in the photo.

32 **1.** If Mr Mackenzie had not been careful, Rebus would have called for assistance.
   2. If the woman in the photograph had been a regular at the bar, someone would have recognised her.
   3. If Rebus had taken the money, he would have bought another orange juice.
   4. If Rebus had left by the fire exit, someone would have been waiting for him in the alley.
   5. If Rebus had been attacked on the street, someone would have called an ambulance.
   6. If Rebus had tried to go back to Mr Mackenzie's office, the fat man would have stopped him.
   7. If the other people admiring the car had been more observant, they would have memorised the number plate.
   8. If the fat man had been more careful, he would have seen Rebus in his car.

33 **1.** aus einem geschlossenen Raum herauskommen: to emerge (herauskommen)
   2. glatt und glänzend: sleek (glatt, glänzend)
   3. ein Fahrzeug eine Zeit lang an einer bestimmten Stelle stehen lassen: to park (abstellen)
   4. gleichwertig sein oder bleiben: to balance (sich ausgleichen, ausgleichen)
   5. ein einziges oder mehrere unterirdische Zimmer in einem Gebäude: basement (Souterrain, Untergeschoss)
   6. etwas für anziehend oder beeindruckend halten: to admire (bewundern)

34 Rebus's friend, Mitch, doesn't join the army because he loses his eye. At first, Rebus keeps in touch with him but after a while he stops writing.
   The next time the casino door opens, eight or nine people leave. Three of them turn in one direction. Rebus follows one of them, pulls over, and invites Matty to come with him for a drive.
   Many of Rebus's colleagues think he is lucky to work in Edinburgh.

35 **1.** The customer asked for a cup of coffee.
   2. Her brother reminds me of my uncle.
   3. The teacher asked us to write about our summer holidays.
   4. Connor was looking for his football in the garden.
   5. I can't stop thinking about you.
   6. My sister doesn't agree with me.

36 **1.** a) Weil es ein entspannter Ort ist.
   2. b) Er überlegt sich, ob er bremsen soll, gibt dann aber Gas.
   3. c) Er fährt langsamer, aber beschleunigt dann wieder.
   4. b) Er erklärt sich bereit, dem Radfahrer ein neues Fahrrad zu kaufen.

37 **1.** Rebus read the sheet through one more time.
   2. He had given Matty two business cards.
   3. Rebus went over the Forth Bridge to Fife.
   4. The police will find Damon.

5. Janis *was* Rebus's girlfriend.

6. Rebus *has dropped* Matty at the foot of Broughton Street.

7. None of the staff at the club *saw* the woman in the photo.

8. Rebus *drinks* orange juice all evening.

9. Rebus *took* Matty for a drive around the town.

10. Siobhan *sat* down at Rebus's table.

11. Matty *has done* the best he can.

12. Matty *shakes* his head.

13. Rebus *will tell* Siobhan about the case.

14. Mr Mackenzie *did* not like Rebus.

38 **1.** Siobhan washes her *muffin* down with milk.

2. Harry is the video *wizard*.

3. Damon is the son of an old *schoolfriend* of Rebus's.

4. Harry is a *great one* for gossip.

5. Rebus brings out the photo from his *pocket*.

6. Rebus was *at the club* last night.

7. Siobhan thinks Rebus was asking the wrong *sex*.

39 **1.** The girls *were bought* a round of drinks by Rebus.

2. A pool table *had been installed* by the owners of the pub.

3. Damon *has not been found* by the police.

4. Mr Mackenzie *has been questioned* by Rebus.

5. The blond woman *was seen* by two men at the club that night.

6. Matty *is driven* around the town by Rebus.

7. The name of the suspect *has been written* down by Matty.

8. Rebus *is asked* by Mrs Playfair about his family.

9. Mr Mackenzie *is being protected* by the bouncer.

10. Rebus *has been joined* at his table by Siobhan.

11. Damon's parents *are told* by Rebus about the case.

12. The Rolls-Royce *had been seen* by Rebus before.

40 **1.** F Die Mädchen erinnern sich nicht daran, die Frau auf dem Foto im Club gesehen zu haben.

2. T *Corinne hat die Frau in der Toilette gesehen, als sie sich schminkte.*

3. F Die Mädchen denken, dass die Frau auf dem Foto nett aussieht.

4. F Corinne bleibt bei Rebus, als die anderen Frauen auf die Toilette gehen.

5. F Rebus fragt Jacky nach ihrer Meinung über den Club.

6. T *Jacky hält Damon für ein bisschen blöd.*

7. F Damons Familie hatte Rebus auch den Eindruck gegeben, dass Damon ein bisschen dumm sei.

8. T *Es wird Rebus klar, dass er nicht viel über Damon weiß.*

9. F Helen und Damon wollen sich verloben.

10. F Helen und Damon stritten sich immer um Geld.

11. T *Die Frau auf dem Foto ist sehr attraktiv gekleidet.*

12. T *Die anderen Frauen sind sehr eifersüchtig auf sie.*

41 **1.** Nobody knew who the woman ~~were~~ **was**.
   2. Jacky asks Rebus if he thinks the woman has ~~gone up~~ **gone off** with Damon.
   3. Jacky doesn't think the woman would have been ~~interesting~~ **interested** in Damon.
   4. Rebus had been promised the fax ~~on~~ **in** the afternoon.
   5. Mr Mandelson ~~don't~~ **doesn't** have a criminal record.
   6. Mr Mandelson used **to** be a casino manager.
   7. The fax gives Rebus a few more facts ~~from~~ **about** Mr Mandelson.
   8. Matty and Stevie ~~was~~ **were** seeing each other socially.
   9. Stevie would sometimes invite Matty ~~to~~ **for** a drink.
   10. Stevie is considered to be the ~~kings~~ **king** of football.
   11. Matty has ~~saw~~ **seen** Stevie in the newspapers.
   12. Stevie misses ~~her~~ **his** schooldays.
   13. Matty can't really ~~remembering~~ **remember** his time at school.
   14. Matty ~~enjoy~~ **enjoys** going out with Stevie.

42 **1.** The kids asked Stevie and Matty for their autographs.
   2. Stevie remembers the teachers' names from school.
   3. They think it is a boring place to grow up.
   4. The girls Stevie brought along for Matty were not as attractive as his own.
   5. Stevie prefers BMWs to Porsches because they have more space for passengers.
   6. The two men don't stay at the club for very long because Stevie has a match the following day.
   7. Stevie drops Matty off outside his flat.
   8. Matty realises that Mr Mandelson's car is parked over the road when he hears the car door opening.
   9. Malibu is Mr Mandelson's driver.
   10. Malibu stands guard after Matty has got into the car.
   11. Mr Mandelson could have bought a secondhand Rolls-Royce before now.
   12. He can afford to buy a new Rolls-Royce now.

43 child – children   table – tables
   story – stories   tooth – teeth
   video – videos   sheep – sheep
   bus – buses   lorry – lorries
   mouse – mice   life – lives
   man – men   foot – feet

44 Matty tells Mr Mandelson that neither he nor Stevie will do as he asks. However, Mr Mandelson has a way to blackmail Matty. He has been contacted by Matty's former employers in **London** who want to find Matty. Mr Mandelson told them he didn't know him but now threatens to tell them where Matty is. Matty threatens to tell them that Mr Mandelson lied and this **makes no impression on** Mr Mandelson. He urges Matty to persuade Stevie not to play well for **one game**.

45 **1.** ein Buch, in dem man Briefmarken usw. aufbewahrt: **album** (Album)
    2. das Kind der Tante oder des Onkels: **cousin** (Cousin, Cousine)
    3. eine Gruppe zwölf identischer Sachen: **dozen** (Dutzend)
    4. eine Gruppe zusammengehöriger Zimmer in einem Stock eines Gebäudes:
       flat (Wohnung)
    5. jemanden erschrecken: **to scare** (erschrecken)
    6. ein Foto, das man schnell macht: **snapshot** (Schnappschuss)

46 **1.** Rebus **is going** to see Brian and Janis.
    2. Brian **was wearing** a smart suit and tie.
    3. Brian and Janis **will be leaving** soon.
    4. They **have been waiting** for news from Rebus.
    5. Janis **had been getting ready** upstairs.
    6. Janis **was coming** downstairs.
    7. Janis **is wearing** a blue dress.
    8. Rebus **will be driving** home soon.

47 **1.** c) Er hat eine andere Verabredung.
    2. a) Sie gibt ihm einen Kuss.
    3. c) Ein Fußballspieler.
    4. b) Die Oxford Bar.

48 drunk   betrunken
     enemy   Feind
     revenge   Rache
     blow   Schlag
     kick   Tritt
     vision   Sehvermögen
     concrete   Beton
     blink   blinzeln
     iron   Eisen
     cemetery   Friedhof
     goal   Tor
     score   schießen
     hero   Held
     team   Mannschaft
     tackle   Angriff

49 **1.** possibility (Möglichkeit) = option
    2. fear (Angst) = panic
    3. occupation (Beschäftigung) = job
    4. quiet (still) = silent
    5. noise (Geräusch) = sound
    6. to ask (fordern) = to demand

50 **1.** They ask him about it.
   2. He is frightened of them.
   3. They invite him to go out dancing.
   4. She helps him with them.
   5. He hasn't written to them.
   6. He gives it to him.

51 **1.** F Raith haben im Moment viel Erfolg.
   2. F Niemand erwartet, dass Stevie ein Tor schießt.
   3. T Herr Mandelson wird wetten, dass das Spiel unentschieden ausgeht.
   4. F Matty wird wegen einer Sache, die er in Glasgow getan hat, erpresst.
   5. T Herrn Mandelsons Angebot interessiert Stevie nicht.
   6. F Stevie öffnet Matty die Tür.
   7. T Herr Mandelson hatte den Füller von jemandem, der ihm Geld schuldete.
   8. F Malibu holt Matty etwas zu trinken.
   9. F Malibu steht neben dem Fenster.
   10. F Matty sagt Herrn Mandelson, dass Stevie sein Angebot abgelehnt hat.
   11. T Matty sagt Herrn Mandelson, dass er lange gebraucht hat, um Stevie zu überreden.
   12. T Malibu und Herr Mandelson sind froh über Mattys Nachricht.

52 **1.** Mr Mandelson sat alone in his office this evening.
   2. Rebus waited quietly outside the door.
   3. Malibu went with a friend to the cinema on Friday.
   4. Janis searched frantically in her handbag.
   5. Stevie played in Kirkcaldy on Saturday.
   6. Malibu waited impatiently in the car.
   7. Brian saw Damon in Bowhill last week.
   8. Rebus drives quickly to Bowhill.
   9. Siobhan saw Rebus at the police station yesterday.
   10. Malibu waits silently in the alley.
   11. Rebus goes to the pub every night.
   12. Rebus telephoned Brian from his office last Friday.

53 **1.** Rebus shook his head.
   2. Cafferty will protect Stevie.
   3. Cafferty has watched all of Stevie's matches.
   4. Cafferty had been a fan of Stevie's.
   5. Rebus and Farmer Watson knew all about Cafferty.
   6. Matty has played a trick on Mandelson.
   7. Matty belongs to Rebus.
   8. Malibu has taken off in the Roller.
   9. Malibu will be a big help.
   10. Rebus saw Mandelson at Gaitanos.
   11. Mandelson chooses Fife for his bets.

12. Mackenzie **had done** some business.

13. Mandelson **has** only one choice.

14. Farmer Watson and Rebus **gave** Mandelson a warning.

54 **1.** All the colour has drained away from Mandelson's **face**.

2. Mandelson's **voice** sounds hollow.

3. Farmer Watson sounds like a kid **unwrapping** his birthday present.

4. It takes Rebus a moment to place Mr Bain's **name**.

5. Rebus had asked Mr Bain to keep an **eye** on Damon's bank account.

6. There have been two **withdrawals** from the account in London.

7. The withdrawal from Finsbury Park was made **two** days ago.

55 **1.** **c)** Weinend und mit geneigtem Kopf.

2. **b)** Seine Schreibarbeit.

3. **a)** Das Trinken einer Tasse Kaffee.

4. **b)** Er tanzt ein bisschen.

56 **1.** Joey knows there's nothing ~~to wait~~ **waiting** for him in his home town.

2. Joey's sister had ~~wrote~~ **written** to him in prison.

3. The news about his wife ~~are~~ **is** bad.

4. Joey had to look ~~after~~ **for** a place to live.

5. The landlord had ~~catched~~ **caught** Joey using the stove as a heater.

6. Joey had tried ~~sleep~~ **sleeping** in the bath.

57 **1.** Joey nearly falls asleep in the library.

2. Joey wakes up when his head hits the book he has been reading.

3. Joey particularly likes the idea in 'The Purloined Letter' about hiding something by putting it right in front of people.

4. The other man in Saughton had committed fraud.

5. According to the man in Saughton, the three things you need to get people to trust you are a suit, a haircut and an expensive watch.

6. By 'the start-up' the man in Saughton had meant money.

7. The old tramp had an unopened newspaper in front of him.

8. The library is so quiet because it is nearly Christmas.

9. Joey finds some notes and coins in the tramp's pocket.

10. Scully Aitchison is campaigning for a central register of offenders.

11. If Scully Aitchison's campaign succeeds, Joey will never get out of the rut he is in.

12. When Rebus sees Jean in Princes Street Gardens she is being hugged by a man dressed as Santa Claus.

58 **1.** Santa moved off just as Rebus ~~were~~ **was** approaching.

2. Jean has a startled look ~~in~~ **on** her face.

3. Jean thinks that the man dressed as Santa Claus has ~~having~~ **had** too much to drink.

4. Jean asks Rebus if he's really going **to** arrest Santa Claus.

5. Rebus isn't looking forward ~~at~~ **to** the evening.

59 Rebus thinks that people will start to relax once they have had a few drinks. He recognises a few of the party guests. One is a journalist and one is a man who he thinks he knows who is here with his **younger** wife. Jean thinks he's an MSP and Rebus confirms that it's Scully Aitchison. Jean says that, according to the information sheet, the **victim** is called Ebenezer Scrooge. Rebus guesses that Aitchison has had a lot to drink. Aitchison announces to everyone that he and his wife have booked a hotel room for the **night**. As **an elderly** lady asks Jean about Little Nell, Rebus spots a man dressed as Santa Claus at the top of the stairs. As he tries to cross the room, Aitchison accuses the man of being the murderer. He gives Scrooge's inhumanity to his fellow man as the reason for the crime. His wife drags him away. Rebus stares at the man dressed as Santa and asks Jean if it's the same one that gave her a hug in the park. Jean **isn't sure because they all look the same**. Rebus watches Santa leave the room and turns back to the other guests. Everyone is now wearing **an item of clothing** to represent their character from Dickens.

60

corridor	Gang
suspicious	misstrauisch
jewellery	Schmuck
wardrobe	Kleiderschrank
bracelet	Armband
tap	leises Klopfen
comment	Bemerkung
dizzy	schwindlig
briefcase	Aktentasche
paperwork	Schreibarbeit
stomach	Magen
jar	Glas
peanut	Erdnuss
law	Recht
sheet	Blatt
salmon	Lachs
envelope	Briefumschlag

61   1. T Der Schauspieler, der Scrooge spielt, liegt auf dem Boden.
   2. F Rebus denkt, er hätte das Verbrechen schon gelöst.
   3. F Rebus sitzt an der Bar und trinkt Wein.
   4. F Jean spricht mit Aitchisons Frau.
   5. T Aitchison glaubt, dass Rebus der Mörder ist.
   6. T Einige Gäste haben angefangen, Magwitch zu befragen.
   7. F Rebus hat den Blick eines aus dem Gefängnis Entlassenen in Miss Havishams Augen gesehen.
   8. F Santa taucht auf und zieht seinen Sack hinter sich her.
   9. F Santa sucht nach Rebus.
  10. T Aitchison behauptet, er würde Santa Claus nicht belügen.
  11. T Santa fragt Aitchison nach seinen Plänen für ein Verzeichnis der Straftäter.
  12. F Aitchisons Neffe sitzt wegen bewaffneten Diebstahls im Gefängnis.

Wörterverzeichnis

about: that's about it das ist alles

account Konto

to acknowledge someone with a nod jemandem zunicken

acquaintance Bekannter, Bekannte

to address someone zu jemandem sprechen

to adjust regeln

admittance Einlass

adulthood Erwachsensein

afresh wieder; von Neuem

afterthought nachträglicher Einfall

to aim something mit etwas zielen

aka (also known as) alias

alive and kicking gesund und munter

all told insgesamt

aloft in die Höhe

to alternate wechselweise tun

ambience Atmosphäre

angle: What is his angle? Was führt er im Schilde?

angled geneigt

to answer the door die Tür aufmachen

apology Entschuldigung

apparent offenkundig

to apply for sich bewerben um

appointment Verabredung

apprentice Lehrling

approval Genehmigung

armpit Achsel

aside außer

as it comes *Getränk* pur

assault tätlicher Angriff

assistance Hilfe

asylum Irrenanstalt

autograph Autogramm

away tie Auswärtsspiel

awkward heikel

aye ja

B&B Frühstückspension, Zimmer mit Frühstück

bank Wand

banking Bankwesen

bank manager Bankfilialleiter(in)

to bark bellen, schnauzen

Barlinnie *Gefängnis in Glasgow*

bar staff Barpersonal

bar stool Barhocker

basement Souterrain

bastard Arschloch

to bawl brüllen

Beamer BMW

bearer *einer Nachricht* Überbringer(in)

to be (was – been) a definite ein klarer Fall sein

to be a great one for gossip eine große Klatschbase sein

to be a laugh Spaß machen

to be a sharp dresser (immer) todschick angezogen sein

to be bogged down festgefahren
sein, überschüttet sein

to be buried begraben sein

to be close to someone mit jemandem eng befreundet sein

to be coming up vor der Tür stehen

to be conducive to something einer
Sache förderlich sein

to be cornered in die Enge
getrieben werden

to be covered geschützt sein

bed and breakfast Frühstückspension, Zimmer mit Frühstück

to be down to whether … darum
gehen, ob …

bedsit möbliertes Zimmer

to be eggshells ein Eiertanz sein

to be family zur Familie gehören

to beg betteln

behalf: on my behalf für mich

to be handy with something mit
etwas gut umgehen können

to be history Geschichte sein

to be hooked by something von
etwas erwischt werden

to be in a clinch with someone von
jemandem umarmt werden

to be in a huddle eng zusammengedrängt sitzen usw.

to be intent on something mit
etwas eifrig beschäftigt sein

to be joking Spaß machen

belch Rülpser

to be made flesh sich erfüllen

to be missing vermisst werden

benevolent fund Unterstützungskasse

to be off out ausgehen

to be on in Ordnung gehen

to be on orange juice Orangensaft
trinken

to be out for someone's blood es auf
jemanden abgesehen haben

to be part and parcel of something
einen wesentlichen Bestandteil
von etwas bilden

to be persuasive jemanden überreden

to be pulling someone's strings
jemanden am Gängelband haben,
jemandes Fäden ziehen

to bequeath hinterlassen

to be raised aufgezogen werden

to be scared turdless eine Scheißangst haben

to be scheming something etwas
aushecken

besides außerdem

to bespeak (bespoke – bespoken)
verraten

best: the best part of a decade fast
ein Jahrzehnt

to be starting out Anfänger(in) sein

bet Wette

to be taken out of the equation *als
Spieler* nicht dabei sein

to be tinged by something einen
Anflug von etwas zeigen

to be trapped in the opposition's
turf in der Fankurve des Gegners
eingeschlossen sein

better: it (had) better das sollte es
besser

to be up against not very much auf
wenig Widerstand stoßen

to be up to something etwas machen

to bide one's time die Zeit abwarten
bigmouth Maulheld
biting *Wind* schneidend
black mark Minuspunkt
to blare out erschallen
to blink back tears seine Tränen
  wegblinzeln
to block someone's way jemandem
  den Weg versperren
bloke Typ
blow Schlag
to blurt something out mit etwas
  herausplatzen
bonnet Haube
book: in my books für mich
bookmaker Buchmacher(in)
to boom dröhnen
to boost erhöhen
to boot someone out jemanden he-
  rausschmeißen
booze Alkohol
to borrow ausleihen
to bother: no one could be bothered
  to … niemand hatte den Nerv …
to bounce aufhüpfen
bouncer Türsteher
to bow one's head den Kopf senken
brace Paar
bracelet Armband
brainy gescheit
brand new nagelneu
break(time) Pause
to break (broke – broken) mitteilen
to break away sich losmachen
to break down zusammenbrechen
to break into a giggle zu kichern
  anfangen

to breathalyse someone jemanden
  ins Röhrchen pusten lassen
to breeze through something ohne
  Schwierigkeiten durch etwas
  durchkommen
brick Bündel
briefcase Aktentasche
brittle zerbrechlich
to broadcast *Nachricht* verbreiten
bruise blauer Fleck
bud Knospe
bugger Arschloch
to bugger off abhauen
building society Bausparkasse
to bunch one's fingers around
  something etwas krallen
to bung something on something
  etwas auf etwas setzen
business card Visitenkarte
busload Busladung
busy unruhig
to buzz someone jemanden anrufen
bystander Zuschauer(in)

to cadge schnorren
candy-floss Zuckerwatte
canny schlau
capacious geräumig
car crash Autounfall
careworn vergrämt
carpeted mit Teppichboden
carrier bag Plastiktüte
to carry on weitermachen
cash Kohle
cashcard Geldautomatenkarte
cash incentive finanzieller Anreiz

cash machine Geldautomat

to cast *Schatten* werfen

casual beiläufig

to catch (caught – caught) oneself
  innehalten

cava Sekt

to cease aufhören

cemetery Friedhof

charge: in charge of verantwortlich
  für

to chase away verjagen

to chat someone up jemanden
  anmachen

to check on someone jemanden
  kontrollieren

cheerio Tschüs

chemo(therapy) Chemotherapie

chief an vorderster Front

chief superintendent Hauptkom-
  missar

ciggie Glimmstängel

children's ward Kinderstation

chip Spielmarke

chisel Meißel

chiselled *Gesicht* kantig

choice zwielichtig

to choke out: he had to choke out
  the words die Worte blieben ihm
  fast im Hals stecken

CID (Criminal Investigation
  Department) Kriminalpolizei

cig(gie) Glimmstängel

circuit Rundreise

to claim behaupten

to clap eyes on someone jemanden
  zu sehen kriegen

clientele Kundschaft

clue Hinweis

clue: I haven't a clue (ich habe)
  keine Ahnung

coastal scenery Küstenlandschaft

to coax überreden

coin-meter Münzzähler

colour: all colour went from his
  face sein Gesicht wurde leichen-
  blass

to come (came – come) bouncing
  up to someone auf jemanden
  munter zukommen

to come down to something auf
  etwas ankommen

to come down: when it comes down
  to it letzten Endes

to come down with a cold sich er-
  kälten

to come off klappen

to come out and ask someone
  something jemanden nach etwas
  offen fragen

to come to aufwachen

to come to a decision zu einem
  Entschluss kommen

come to that eigentlich

to come to trial vor Gericht kommen

to come up with something etwas
  entdecken, sich etwas einfallen
  lassen

comment Bemerkung

commentary Kommentar

commerce Handel

community Gemeinschaft

compensation Entschädigung

competition Konkurrenz

complex kompliziert

computer-enhanced computerver-
  bessert

concrete Beton

to confront someone jemandem gegenübertreten

conscientious gewissenhaft

consciousness Bewusstsein

constabulary Polizei

constituency Wahlkreis

to continue fortfahren

convicted verurteilt

cop car Streifenwagen

corridor Gang

council estate gemeindeeigene Wohnsiedlung

to cover someone jemanden decken

cracker toller Mann; tolle Frau

crank Spinner(in)

to crimp wellen

to crouch hocken

cruise liner Kreuzfahrtschiff

crumpled zerknittert

crush Gedränge

crutch Stütze

crystal ball Kristallkugel

curling tongs Lockenstab

currency Währung

current account Girokonto

cushy ruhig, gemütlich

daft blöd

dance floor Tanzfläche

to dart around hin und her huschen

DC (Detective Constable) Kriminalwachtmeister(in)

dead verlassen

deal: Have we got a deal? Abgemacht?

to deal (dealt – dealt) out *Spielkarten* geben

decade Jahrzehnt

to deduct abziehen

definition Bildschärfe

delay: there was a delay es verspätete sich

dense begriffsstutzig

desire Wunsch

despair Verzweiflung

destination Reiseziel

detective sergeant Polizeimeister

Dickensian Dickens'sch

diddle Betrug

dimly lit schwach beleuchtet

to dine essen

diner *im Restaurant* Gast

dinner-dance Abendgesellschaft mit Tanz

dinner money Essensgeld

discreet diskret

disenchantment Desillusionierung

to disgorge ausspeien

disgust: in disgust angewidert

to dislodge lösen

dismissive abweisend

distinct from anders als

distinction Unterschied

distraction Ablenkung

to ditch wegschmeißen

dizzy schwindlig

dockyard Werft

doll Tussi

done: it was the done thing das war eben so üblich

to do (did – done) a runner abhauen, zu Fuß flüchten

to do a U-turn wenden

to doodle kritzeln

to do one's damnedest sich alle
Mühe geben

to do one's eyes sich die Augen
schminken

to do/serve time (im Gefängnis)
sitzen

to do some ferreting herumschnüffeln

to do someone a favour jemandem
einen Gefallen tun

doorman Türsteher

to double as something sich auch
als etwas verwenden lassen

doubly doppelt

down-and-out Penner(in)

down-payment Anzahlung

down south im Süden

dream: like a dream traumhaft

dreary trüb

dressed to kill aufgedonnert

to drift *Blick* wandern

drink: a drink to show for the long
wait ein Drink als Ergebnis der
langen Warterei

to drop absetzen

to drop by vorbeikommen

to drop in vorbeischauen

drop-in centre Treffpunkt für Obdachlose usw.

to drop something back to someone
etwas bei jemandem vorbeibringen

drowning man Ertrinkender

drunk betrunken

drunk driving Trunkenheit am
Steuer

dry-mouthed: he felt dry-mouthed
sein Mund wurde trocken

duff beschissen

dugout Trainerbank

to dump out wegschmeißen

to dump someone jemanden fallen
lassen

duration: for the duration während
dieser Zeit

to ease off nachlassen

to ease off the accelerator
langsamer fahren

to ease oneself out sich heraushieven

easy immer mit der Ruhe

edge Vorteil

to edit something down to another
tape etwas schneiden und auf ein
anderes Video übertragen

elated in Hochstimmung

to emerge from one's seat aussteigen

to encircle umringen

to end up at schließlich landen in

to end up doing something
schließlich etwas machen

enemy Feind(in)

engaged verlobt

engagement ring Verlobungsring

to entertain people Gäste haben

envelope Briefumschlag

to erase auslöschen

evening session Abend

eventually schließlich

to eye schauen auf

face: to someone's face offiziell

to fade ausbleichen

fair: more than fair recht gut

fair point stimmt

faith Vertrauen

fancy dress shop Kostümladen

fare Fahrgast

farewell Abschied

fart Furz

feature *Gesicht* Zug

to feel (felt – felt) queasy ein Gefühl der Übelkeit haben

fellow man Mitmensch

festive spirit feierliche Stimmung

fiction Romane

fierce erbittert

to file one's copy seinen Bericht schreiben

to file something away etwas im Gedächtnis ablegen

to fill a gap eine Lücke füllen

final-whistle Schlusspfiff

fire Heizgerät

fire exit Notausgang

five feet four 1,62 m

fixture Spiel

flat out ausgestreckt

flattered geschmeichelt

flaw Fehler

flight of stairs Treppe

the Flintstones Familie Feuerstein

to flip through durchblättern

to flit over: his eyes flitted over it er überflog es mit den Augen

flyer Flugblatt

food trolley Einkaufswagen

football pools Toto

frame *Film* Einzelbild

fraud Betrug

fraudster Betrüger(in)

to freeze(-frame) (froze – frozen) *Film* anhalten

to frown die Stirn runzeln

frown: a frown on his face stirnrunzelnd

to fuck: he can fuck himself er kann mich mal

to fuck up Scheiß machen

to fuck with someone jemanden verarschen, sich in jemandes Angelegenheiten einmischen

full-length bodenlang

to fumble through something etwas durchwühlen

furious wütend

to fuss for something nach etwas umständlich suchen

fuzzy unscharf, verschwommen

G

gaffer Vorarbeiter

gambler Glücksspieler

games *Schulfach* Sport

gaming licence Glücksspielerlaubnis

gaze Blick

gee-gee *Kindersprache* Pferd

genius-in-waiting zukünftiges Genie

to get (got – got): he didn't get it er hat es nicht verstanden

to get away with it sich alles erlauben können

to get back to someone about something auf jemanden wegen etwas zurückkommen, jemanden wegen etwas zurückrufen

to get engaged sich verloben

to get in touch sich melden

to get one's head straight seinen Kopf freibekommen

to get one's round in eine Runde schmeißen

to get out of a rut aus einem Trott herauskommen

to get round to doing something dazu kommen, etwas zu tun

to get something in etwas kaufen

to get something over with etwas hinter sich bringen

to get the nerve up den Mut fassen

to get together zusammenkommen

to get to one's feet aufstehen

to get to the point zur Sache kommen

gift Gabe

to girn meckern

to give (gave – given) someone a bell jemanden anrufen

to give someone a good hiding jemandem eine ordentliche Tracht Prügel verpassen

to give someone grief jemandem Kummer machen

to give someone the once-over jemanden mit einem Blick abschätzen

to glance towards flüchtig blicken auf

to glint funkeln

gloss-black glänzend schwarz

to go (went – gone) down to gehen nach/ins

to go for something sich für etwas bereit erklären

to go in hard hart angreifen

to go through a bad patch *als Fußballmannschaft* im Moment nicht besonders gut spielen

goal Tor

goalkeeper Torwart

goalless torlos

gorgeous hübsch

to grab something nach etwas greifen

to grace mit seiner Anwesenheit beehren

graceful elegant

grain of sand Sandkorn

graze Abschürfung

greasy schmierig

to grow (grew – grown) flushed erröten

to growl *Magen* knurren

to guess annehmen

gut: he doesn't have the guts ihm fehlt der Schneid

to hand down weitergeben

to hand over übergeben

to harbour suspicions einen Verdacht haben

hard knallhart

to haul ziehen

to have (had – had) a buzz on betrunken sein

to have a criminal record vorbestraft sein

to have a finger in something mit etwas zu tun haben

to have an early night früh ins Bett gehen

to have a stab at something etwas versuchen

to have someone pegged a crank jemanden als Spinner abstempeln

to have something for company
  von etwas begleitet sein; etwas als
  Gesellschaft haben
to have something in mind etwas
  im Sinn haben
to head back zurückgehen, zurück-
  fahren
to head off losgehen, losfahren
to head up die Treppe hinaufgehen
head office Hauptgeschäftsstelle
headstone Grabstein
to heave kotzen
heaving brechend voll
Heavy night? Zu viel getrunken
  gestern Abend?
hefty gewaltig
heart: his heart is in the right place
  er hat das Herz auf dem rechten
  Fleck
heart: his heart sank der Mut ver-
  ließ ihn
height: at the height of auf dem
  Höhepunkt
here we go jetzt geht's los
hero Held
hey presto Simsalabim
to highlight hervorheben
highly thought of hochgeschätzt
high roller Spieler, der um hohe
  Einsätze spielt
hitch(hik)ing Trampen, per Anhalter
  fahren
to hold (the line) (held – held) am
  Apparat bleiben
to hold back verheimlichen
hollow hohl
home draw Heimunentschieden
home game Heimspiel

to hook up with someone sich
  jemandem anschließen
host Wirt, Gastgeber
hostel Wohnheim
house Haus (Firma)
housebreaker Einbrecher
to hover sich in der Nähe aufhalten
How come …? Wie kommt es,
  dass …?
How much are you in for? Wie viel
  willst du einsetzen?
hug Umarmung
humility Demut

I

imp Lausbub
impish schelmisch
incentive: as an incentive als Anreiz
inclined: he's not that way inclined
  das ist nicht sein Fall
incorrigible unverbesserlich
to indulge in something sich etwas
  gönnen
inextricable untrennbar
inhumanity Unmenschlichkeit
initial erste, erster, erstes
injured verletzt
inlaid eingelegt
inscription Inschrift
to insist beharren
inspection Prüfung
inspector Kommissar
to install hineinstellen
interest-bearing account Sparkonto
interior light Innenbeleuchtung;
  inneres Licht
interior lighting Innenbeleuchtung

to introduce someone to someone
jemand jemandem vorstellen
in vain vergeblich
inward-looking nach innen gewandt
Irn-Bru *eine Art Limo*
iron Eisen

J'accuse! Sie sind schuldig!
jagged *Bewegung* jäh
jail Gefängnis
jar Glas
jaunty: at a jaunty angle schief aufgesetzt
jealousy Eifersucht
jewellery Schmuck
to jimmy open aufstemmen
to join: Mind if I join you? Darf ich
mich zu dir setzen?
to join the army zum Militär gehen
jokey scherzhaft
judgment Urteilsvermögen
to jump through hoops schaulaufen

to keep (kept – kept) a low profile
sich zurückhalten
to keep an eye open for something
nach etwas Ausschau halten
to keep guard Wache stehen
to keep tabs on something ein
wachsames Auge auf etwas haben
keepie-up Ball-Jonglieren
kerb(side) Randstein
kick Tritt
to kill for something für etwas alles
geben

kit Sachen
kitchen-stool haircut von der Mutter geschnittene Haare
to knife someone jemanden nieder-
stechen
to knock someone unconscious jemanden k.o. schlagen
to knock something off something
etwas um etwas herabsetzen
to knot binden
knuckle Knöchel

lad Junge
lager helles Bier
laid-back gelassen
landing Flur
landlord Vermieter
landmark Wahrzeichen
last time I looked so weit ich weiß
latterday der Gegenwart
law Recht
law-abiding gesetzestreu
to lay (laid – laid) out einsetzen
to lean forward sich vorbeugen
to leap to one's feet aufspringen
to learn the ropes sich einarbeiten
leave Urlaub
leper Aussätzige(r)
lesson Lehre
to let (let – let) oneself out hinaus-
gehen
to let out zumachen
lifeblood Lebensader
lifeless leblos
to lift klauen
like: and the like und so weiter
line Witz

to linger bei einem Gedanken verweilen

loan material Material zum Ausleihen

lobby Flur

local Einheimischer, Einheimische; Leute vor Ort

locally am Ort

to lock something up etwas unter Dach und Fach bringen

to look for a needle in a haystack eine Nadel im Heuhaufen suchen

to loom over something über etwas aufragen

to loosen lockern

to lose (lost – lost) count den Überblick verlieren

to lose one's eye sein Auge verlieren

lot: the lot alles

low-ceilinged mit tief sitzender Decke

to lumber off sich trampelnd wegbewegen

lunchtime *Schule* große Pause

made good erfolgreich

to make (made – made) a gamble with someone mit jemandem eine Wette eingehen

to make something count etwas nutzen

to make towards someone sich jemandem nähern

malt Malt Whisky

manager Filialleiter(in)

marker *Spiel* Manndecker(in)

marker *Text* Leuchtstift

to master beherrschen

mate Kumpel

matter: no matter what ganz egal, was passiert

mean kärglich

meantime inzwischen

mellow angeheitert

memento Andenken

memorial Denkmal

to memorise sich einprägen

Merc Mercedes

merely bloß

to mess up schmutzig machen

to mete out zumessen

mezzanine floor Zwischengeschoss

to milk melken

to mime pantomimisch darstellen

mind (you) allerdings

mind: he didn't seem to mind es schien ihm nichts auszumachen

Miners' Institute Freizeitzentrum für Bergleute

to mingle sich mischen

mining tragedy Grubenunglück

minor klein, geringfügig

MisPers Vermisste

missing person Vermisster, Vermisste

to mistreat schlecht behandeln

m'lud (=my lord) Euer Gnaden

mogul Magnat

to mooch around herumlungern

mood: if the mood takes me wenn ich dazu aufgelegt bin

more like eher

moron Schwachkopf

to motion winken

to motion for someone to go in jemanden hineinwinken

motoring offence Verkehrsdelikt

to move in on something sich
näher an etwas stellen

MSP Mitglied des schottischen Parlaments

to muffle dämpfen

nag Pferd

name-tag Namensschild

National Lottery Lotto

to necessitate erfordern

nee geborene

nepotism Vetternwirtschaft

news: it's news to me das ist mir
neu

nick (kleine) Schnittwunde

nicked eingekerbt

nickname Spitzname

nightwatch Nachtwache

no-alcohol alkoholfrei

no' bad (= not bad) nicht schlecht

to nod off einnicken

note Entschuldigung

notion Idee

nude mag Nacktmagazin

number plate Kennzeichen

occupation Beschäftigung

odds Gewinnchancen

odds: the odds will be on you scoring
man wird darauf wetten, dass du
ein Tor schießt

off: off South Clerk Street in einer
Querstraße zur South Clerk
Street

offender Straftäter, Verbrecher

Old Firm match *Fußballspiel zwischen Celtic und Rangers*

on: eleven months on elf Monate
später

on: on green/red bei Grün/Rot

on: that's not on das ist nicht akzep-
tabel

on you go now du kannst jetzt gehen

one-note wonder Mensch, der nur
ein Talent hat

one-one 1:1

onlooker Zuschauer(in)

on-the-town clothes feine Klamotten

optic Portionierer

our best bet is höchstens

out cold bewusstlos

out of place fehl am Platz

outsider Fremder, Fremde

overcast bewölkt

overdue überfällig

to overstretch oneself sich über-
nehmen

to owe schulden

packet ein Haufen Geld

pal Freund(in)

palm Handfläche

palpable spürbar

paper: on paper auf dem Papier

paperwork Schreibarbeit

parking warden Politesse

particular: to him in particular ausgerechnet ihm

party atmosphere Partystimmung

to pass away entschlafen

patch Revier

to pay (paid – paid) off gelingen

payment Zahlung

peace: at peace ruhig

peanut Erdnuss

to peck someone on the cheek jemandem einen flüchtigen Kuss auf die Wange geben

percentage Anteil

percentage: there is little percentage in it es bringt nichts

to perch sitzen

person: in person persönlich

pet Schatz

petty thief kleiner Dieb

to pick out auswählen

to pick up lernen

to pine away vor Gram vergehen

to place one's bet wetten, setzen

to place someone in his mid-fifties schätzen, dass jemand Mitte fünfzig ist

to place the face ein Gesicht zuordnen

to place the name einen Namen zuordnen

plague of boils Eiterbeulenpest

platinum platinblond

plenty enough mehr als genug

plumbing Klempnerarbeiten

plush elegant

to ply someone with booze jemanden zum Trinken nötigen

to pocket something etwas in die eigene Tasche stecken

pockmarked pockennarbig

point on the compass Himmelsrichtung

to point somebody out to somebody jemandem jemanden zeigen

poke *Geschlechtsverkehr* Nummer

pontoon 17 und 4

to pop in vorbeikommen

to pore over eifrig studieren

portrait Bild

to pose posieren

posh vornehm

post Posten

to post bekanntgeben

post-dated vordatiert

powder-blue taubenblau

precious little herzlich wenig

prefab Fertighaus

premises Gebäude

pressure Druck

price: whatever the price um jeden Preis

to prickle zusammenzucken

privacy Privatleben

to proceed to trial gerichtlich vorgehen

procurator fiscal Staatsanwalt (in Schottland)

prom(enade) Strandpromenade

prominence: of prominence auffällig

prominent *Zähne* vorstehend

prosperous wohlhabend

to prowl herumschleichen (in)

to psych out erkennen

public öffentlich

puddled alley Gasse voller Pfützen

puff: in a puff of smoke wie vom Erdboden verschluckt

to puff out aufblasen

pull Anziehungskraft

to pull a job ein Ding drehen

to pull a scheme ein Ding drehen

to pull over zur Seite fahren

punch Schlag

punchline Pointe

punter Kunde, Kundin; Kerl

punters queuing three deep mit
Kunden brechend voll

to purchase kaufen

purloined gestohlen

to push a number *Telefon* wählen

to push the accelerator Gas geben

to put (put – put) a proposition to
someone jemandem einen Vor-
schlag machen

to put names to faces Namen in Verbindung mit Gesichtern bringen

to put one's foot down Gas geben

to put one's head round the door
den Kopf zur Tür hereinstecken

to put one's mind to something
über etwas scharf nachdenken

to put someone away jemanden
einsperren

to put someone off something
jemandem etwas verleiden

to put someone's mind at rest
jemanden beruhigen

to put something behind one etwas
hinter sich bringen

to put the phone down auflegen

to put up aufhängen

quid Pfund

railings Zaun

Raith (Rovers) *Fußballklub in Kirkcaldy*

ransom Lösegeld

to rat on someone jemanden ver-
pfeifen

to read (read – read) up on sich
einlesen in

to reason argumentieren

to reassure someone of something
jemandem etwas versichern

receiver Hörmuschel

recent neu

to recruit einstellen

to redeem ausgleichen

redemption: beyond redemption
hoffnungslos verloren

red-suited in einem roten Anzug

to reel off herunterrasseln

to regain one's composure seine
Selbstbeherrschung wiederfinden

regular Stammgast

release Entlassung

to relent nachgeben

relief Erleichterung

remedy Heilmittel

to remind someone of something
jemanden an etwas erinnern

remote (control) Fernbedienung

to replace ersetzen

residential street Wohnstraße

residual zurückgeblieben

to rest hängenbleiben

to retain the championship wieder
Meister werden

retina Netzhaut

to retreat sich zurückziehen

retribution Strafe

to reveal oneself as something sich
als etwas zu erkennen geben

revenge Rache

ringmaster Zirkusdirektor

to ripple trudeln

to rise (rose – risen) to one's feet aufstehen

roaming beweglich

to roar away losbrausen

Roller Rolls-Royce

room: put it on my room setzen Sie es auf meine Zimmerrechnung

room service Zimmerservice

to rub reiben

rubble Trümmer

to run (ran – run) organisieren

to run a red light eine rote Ampel überfahren

runaway Ausreißer(in)

to run out ausgehen

to run rings around someone jemanden in die Tasche stecken

run-up to Christmas Vorweihnachtszeit

rusty aus der Übung

S

salmon Lachs

Samaritan: good Samaritan barmherziger Samariter

sandpaper Schmirgelpapier

sanity clause Zurechnungsfähigkeitsklausel

SAS *Spezialeinheit der britischen Armee*

satchel Schulranzen

Saughton Jail *Gefängnis in Edinburgh*

to saunter in hineinschlendern, hereinschlendern

to save: it saved (on) (him) having to do something es hat ihm erspart, etwas tun zu müssen

scam Betrügerei

scene: behind the scenes hinter den Kulissen

scented from heaven and all stations south hochgradig parfümiert

to score *Tor* schießen, erzielen

season ticket Dauerkarte

sec Moment

second: we put ourselves second (to him) er hat bei uns an erster Stelle gestanden

secondhand aus zweiter Hand

security Wachpersonal

to see (saw – seen) one another socially sich privat treffen

select ausgewählt

to self-destruct sich selbst zerstören

self-satisfied selbstgefällig

sense of community Gemeinschaftssinn

sentiment Sentimentalität

to serve time im Gefängnis sitzen

to settle in es sich gemütlich machen

sex Geschlecht

sex goddess Sexbombe

to shake (shook – shaken) one's head den Kopf schütteln

shakily wacklig

shark Hai

to shed ablegen

to shed one's disguise seine Verkleidung ablegen

sheet *Papier* Blatt

to shelter sich unterstellen

to shift sich unruhig hin und her bewegen; wechseln

shift Schicht

shift changeover Schichtwechsel

shopkeeper Ladenbesitzer(in)

shortage of Mangel an

short-sighted kurzsichtig

to shrug mit den Schultern zucken

to shrug off ignorieren

to shuffle sich über die Tanzfläche schieben, schlurfen

sign: there's no sign of him er ist nirgendwo zu sehen

to signal blinken

to sit tight warten

to skew verzerren

to skid schleudern

to skin someone alive jemandem den Kopf abreißen

to skive off schwänzen

to slap down hinschmeißen

sleeping partner stiller Teilhaber

slicked back geschniegelt

to sling something over one's shoulder etwas über die Schulter schmeißen

to slip one's hand into something die Hand heimlich in etwas stecken

to slope off abhauen

to slouch latschen

slumped zusammengesackt

small-arms Handfeuerwaffen

smart-casual sportlich elegant

to smirk grinsen

to snap schnauzen

to sniff schniefen

to sniff around herumschnüffeln

snitch Denunziant(in)

snobby versnobt

to soak up *Erlebnis* aufsaugen

sodium Natrium

soft drink alkoholfreies Getränk

something like that so ungefähr

to sound one's horn hupen

span of time Zeitspanne

Speaking. Am Apparat.

spectator Zuschauer(in)

spiel Sprüche

spirit guide Geisterführer

to spit: it makes me spit es kotzt mich an

to spot entdecken

to spread something around etwas verteilen

to squeeze (oneself) in sich hineinzwängen

to stack sich stapeln

stack Regal

staff Personal

stake Einsatz

to stand about ... ... groß sein

to stand half a chance eine halbe Chance haben

startled überrascht

stash Vorrat

station *Polizei* Wache

to stave off lindern

stays Korsett

to steep in the bath sich im Bad einweichen

to step on (someone's) toes jemandem auf den Schlips treten

to stick around dableiben

still Standbild

stitching Naht

to stock füllen

stomach Magen

to stoop sich bücken

stove Herd

straight off sofort

strapless schulterfrei

stuck-up hochnäsig

studs-first mit den Stollen voraus

stuffy muffig

to stumble into something in etwas aus Versehen geraten

sub-committee Unterausschuss

subject Untertan(in)

such as zum Beispiel

superficial oberflächlich

suppose: I suppose so. Ich denke schon.

surveillance Überwachung

suspicious misstrauisch

to suss (out) dahinterkommen

to swallow hinunterschlucken

sward Rasen

to swear (swore – sworn) schwören

sweetie Süßer, Süße

to swish wirbeln

tab Rechnung

tabloid Boulevardzeitung

tackle Angriff

to take (took – taken): she didn't take it that way sie verstand es nicht so

to take a beating von etwas erwischt werden, eine Schlappe einstecken

to take a deep breath tief Luft holen

to take a left nach links abbiegen

to take a soak ein Bad nehmen

to take off abhauen

to take over from someone jemanden ablösen

to take sips of something an etwas nippen

to tap klopfen

tap leises Klopfen

Teacher's *Whiskymarke*

team Mannschaft

teens: in one's teens im Teenager-alter

to teeter schwanken

tenement Mietshaus

tension Spannung

terrace *im Stadion* Rang

textbook Lehrbuch

that in itself was reminder enough allein das war Erinnerung genug

there, there na, komm

thick doof

thing: the thing is … die Sache ist die …

to think (thought – thought) of oneself as something sich für etwas halten

thirty-odd years gut dreißig Jahre

thou Riesen (= Tausend)

thoughtless rücksichtslos

three-card brag *Kartenspiel*

throng Menschenmenge

to throw (threw – thrown) a party eine Party schmeißen

to throw something in etwas extra dazugeben

to thump someone's arm jemandem am Arm einen Schlag versetzen

timer Uhr

to tiptoe out sich davonstehlen aus

toe-rag Depp

toll Mautgebühr

to top up nachfüllen

torchlight Schein einer Taschen-
lampe
tow: in tow with zusammen mit
to wit nämlich
toxic voller Gift
trainee Auszubildender, Auszu-
bildende
tramp Penner(in)
to transfer übertragen
tricked out geschmückt
troublesome schwierig
trouble-strewn voller Schwierigkeiten
to trust someone jemandem trauen
to try it on with someone versuchen,
wie weit man mit jemandem gehen
kann; es bei jemandem versuchen
tub Badewanne
to tug heftig ziehen
turf Revier
turn: a turn of the cards das Umdrehen der Karten
to turn someone away jemanden
fortschicken
to turn the clock back die Zeit
zurückdrehen
to turn to something sich einer
Sache zuwenden
to tweak ändern
twenty Zwanziger
to twist drehen
twitchy unruhig

umpteenth: for the umpteenth
time zum x-ten Mal
unbidden unaufgefordert
to unfold sich entwickeln

uniform uniformierter Polizist/
Wachposten
Union Jack *britische Nationalflagge*
unlikely unwahrscheinlich
to unwrap auswickeln
up-to-date aktuell

valuables Wertsachen
to vary ändern
vetting procedure Überprüfung
vice Laster
vicinity Nähe
Victorian viktorianisch
villain Verbrecher(in), Übeltäter(in)
virgin Jungfrau
visibly sichtlich
vision Sehvermögen
to visit the loo aufs Klo gehen
voice: a raised voice ein lautes Wort

to wade in sich einmischen
to wag a finger at someone drohend
den Finger gegenüber jemandem
erheben
to walk a circuit of something um
etwas gehen
walking-tour Rundgang
to wander over hinübergehen
want Wunsch
want: 'Okay', he said, for want of anything better „Okay" sagte er, weil
ihm nichts Besseres einfiel.
wardrobe Kleiderschrank
wary vorsichtig
to wash something down etwas hi-
nunterspülen

watertight wasserdicht
way outside weit außerhalb
to weave torkeln
wee klein
well-built kräftig
well-heeled gut betucht
What's in it for him? Was hat er davon?
wheel: behind the wheel am Steuer
to wheel schieben
wheezing keuchend
whereabouts Verbleib
white-hot priority höchste Priorität
the whole works der ganze Krempel
to wind (wound – wound) down
one's window das Fenster her-
unterkurbeln
to wipe löschen
withdrawal Abhebung
witness Zeuge, Zeugin
wizard Genie
whoah halt
woodwork Tischlerei
woolly suit uniformierter Polizist
word is going around es spricht
sich herum
to work klappen
to work a treat ein Riesenerfolg sein
to work oneself up into a state sich
aufregen
to worry zerren
to worry oneself sleepless sich
Sorgen machen, bis man nicht
mehr schlafen kann
worse for wear angetrunken
to wriggle zappeln
to writhe sich krümmen

to yack quasseln
years back vor Jahren
to yield to something einer Sache
weichen

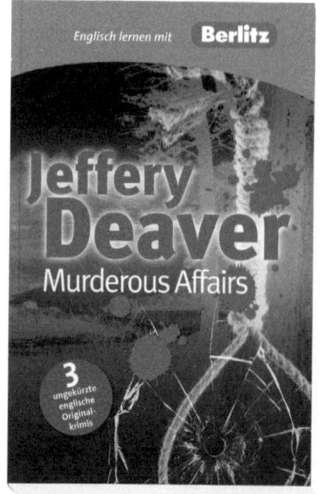

Vom Anfänger **Berlitz** ®
zum Superhero

„Heldenhaftes Englisch" mit Superman und Batman garantieren die neuen Berlitz Comic-Lektüren. Dank der Ausklappseiten mit Vokabelerklärungen und der Comic-Bilder können bereits fortgeschrittene Anfänger den englischen Originaltext leicht verstehen und beim entspannten Comic-Schmökern ihre Sprachkenntnisse verbessern.

Berlitz
Englisch lernen mit Superman
Up, up and away!

Berlitz
Englisch lernen mit Batman
Bad Guys Gallery

Infos & mehr